THE COLLEGE SUCCESS CHEAT SHEET

Simple Ideas to Help You Study Less and Learn More

JONATHAN LEE DAVIDSON

First Printing 2015

ISBN-13: 978-1514858134
ISBN-10: 1514858134

www.collegesuccesscheatsheet.com

Printed in the United States of America

Contents

Introduction vi

Chapter One
Using the Spacing Effect to Study Less and Learn More 1

Chapter Two
Use Surveying to Review Textbook Chapters In Ten Minutes or Less 7

Chapter Three
How to Crush Math, Double Your Reading Speed, Take Notes and Own English 13

Chapter Four
Unleash Boundless Creativity and Build a Knowledge Base 27

Chapter Five
The Art and Science of Science 36

Chapter Six
Taking Tests: Tips from Beyond the Realm of Preparation 43

Chapter Seven
Small College Hacks That Make a Big Difference 50

Chapter Eight
Use Sleep, Exercise, and Diet to Keep Your Head Clear (Literally), Get Straight A's, and Avoid the Freshman Fifteen 63

Chapter Nine
How to Use Internet, Campus, and Student Resources 73

Chapter Ten
How to Increase Personal Productivity Without Burning Out 82

Chapter Eleven
How to Enjoy College 86

Chapter Twelve
Finding Work During or After College 95

Afterword 101

Acknowledgments 102

Crib Notes 103

Bibliography 112

This book is dedicated to Mrs. Snow, who taught me how to write, and to my wife, who lets me.

Introduction

Why You Need This Book

Some students study hard and excel. Some study the same amount and struggle or even fail. Others choose not to study and therefore fail, but if you're in this category, this book isn't for you.

If you're anything like me, you fall into the second category. You do the examples, read the chapters, and fill out the worksheets. Yet when you take a test, the knowledge you worked so hard for hides in the dark crevasses of your mind, just outside the light of consciousness. You struggle through tests with your muscles tight, your breathing shallow, and a cold cannonball sitting in your stomach. Despite all the work and worry, you fall short of the grade you desired—or you even fail.

You might be tempted to feel that some students are just smarter than you. After all, those students put in the same amount of effort—or maybe less—than you did, and yet they do well in their academics. But in my journey from failing many classes in my first year at a community college to being the sole recipient of the President's Award upon my graduation from a private university, I learned that intelligence has little to do with grades.

The difference between great students and everyone else is in how those great students study. And the good news is this: If you learn and faithfully apply the best study techniques used by great students, you too will join their ranks.

Unfortunately, school systems and most universities don't teach good study techniques. If anything, professors and other students will tell you to highlight important stuff in your textbook, make flashcards, or read your homework out loud. But these aren't the study techniques that will transform your college experience from an anxiety-riddled chore to a journey that brings you the confidence born of crushing your exams, papers, and projects.

Great students may use some of the simpler study techniques, but the real secret to their academic success isn't color-coded highlights. Consciously or unconsciously, they use powerful study techniques like *the spacing effect* and *surveying* to help them efficiently learn and retain vast amounts of information.

This book will teach you the techniques and patterns of behavior that power great students. These techniques and behaviors took me from failure to success, and I am confident that if you apply them faithfully, you too can change your academic future.

Failing

I always thought I was smart. Not Einstein smart, but smart enough to handle normal life, and certainly college.

I was wrong.

The trouble started in my first semester of community college. I didn't understand math—I failed algebra five times and statistics once—but lots of smart people can't do math, right?

Despite having earned decent grades in high school, I was failing college—even though I studied for hours more than some of my classmates. In addition to failing math, I was barely passing music theory—even though I was a lead guitarist in a band—and struggling in my other classes. I did well in English because I loved to read, but everything else was dragging my GPA through the mud. I finished my first year of college with a transcript littered with D, F, and W grades, and several classes to retake. My GPA for the classes I actually passed was a 2.5. At this rate, it would take me several extra years to finish my degree with a decent GPA.

Being so overwhelmed humbled me. Obviously, I wasn't nearly as smart as I had believed. Quitting college wasn't an option in my mind, so there was only one thing to do: study harder.

I read every page of assigned reading two or three times. I did extra math problems and completed every assignment long before its due date. It worked: My grades improved and I failed fewer classes.

But I began to hate college. The thought of spending the next three and a half years of my life as a slave to homework, spending all my spare time studying, was depressing. On the other hand, so was the thought of going through life without a college degree. I resigned myself to enduring the remainder of my enslavement, telling myself that it was for the best.

A New Hope

A psychology professor named Lisa rescued me. She told my class about the spacing effect, a study technique that saved her life in graduate school.

I immediately applied the spacing effect to my studies, and my grades started to improve. I stopped failing classes, though I still wasn't where I wanted to be in life. I wanted the freedom to enjoy my hobbies and still get a near-perfect GPA. Now that I understood the spacing effect, I knew this was possible.

Soon after learning about the spacing effect, I discovered and modified a textbook-reading method known as SQ3R. SQ3R by itself leads to a 10-15% better retention rate of studied material. When I combined my modified version of SQ3R, called surveying, with the spacing effect, I realized I'd found a true game-changer in the way I approached studying.

Learning and applying these two techniques helped me maintain a 3.9 GPA for the next three years of college. Almost instantly I escaped the drudgery of cramming and stressing and not having much to show for it. The feeling was indescribable. I could study half the amount I'd studied when I was failing yet earn near-perfect grades.

I love finding the easy way out of difficult situations and succeeding in those endeavors at the same time. Researching study techniques became my addiction. I talked to professors and top students, and I scoured the Internet. I found several more killer techniques and developed a study system that combined them all in sweet harmony. The various techniques reinforced one another and led to powerful, thorough learning.

The Results

I knew that I was onto something big when I first started using my new study system, but I had no idea just how much it would help me accomplish. Two years ago, I graduated with my undergraduate degree from La Sierra University, a private liberal arts school in Riverside, California, and received the President's Award—the highest award the university gives to a graduating student. From my first year of college to my last, my GPA climbed from a 2.5 to a 3.6, and the cumulative GPA for my three years at La Sierra was a 3.9.

But even better than this was the way using college success principles gave me enough time to pursue passions outside of college. Even though I spent a lot of time studying, during my last three years of college I day-hiked Mt. Whitney, the tallest mountain in the contiguous United States, three times. I wrote a one hundred thousand-word novel and got around forty thousand words into two others. I sold several articles to business consulting firms and wrote most of this book. I remodeled and rented out two houses and launched a language teaching business on www.kickstarter.com. I performed over 150 concerts in fifteen states with my men's chorus. I also got married, regularly went mountain biking, took voice lessons, and stayed active in my church.

I was able to do so much because I had extra time. That's the invaluable gift that proper study techniques can give you. Once you have time, you can pursue your dreams.

I once saw a sign that said, "ATTENTION: don't leave your longings unattended." Four years of college can feel extremely long and arduous if you check your longings at the admissions office. If you faithfully follow the college success principles in this book, you too will have time to pursue your dreams while still dominating your GPA. These should be some of the best years of your life. Don't waste them with inefficient studying.

The Greatest Secret

Proper study techniques will go a long way toward helping you excel in college, but there's a specific trait that you must possess in order to wield their true power.

Let's say there are two college students. One has an IQ of 140. The other has an IQ of 100 but has to raise two kids by herself and desperately wants a better life for them. If asked to bet on who would do better in college, I would bet on the motivated student with an average IQ every time.

If you really want to get the most out of college, you have to be motivated. But how can you motivate yourself? There are two ways: by actively finding your gratitude and by thinking toward a compelling future.

If you're going to college, you're privileged. Billions of people will never have this opportunity and would do anything to trade places with you. You'll live a longer, wealthier, more socially conscious life, and you may have extra time and money to enjoy yourself. What an extraordinary blessing. Don't squander it. Be profoundly grateful every single day that you're going to college. Take time to allow gratitude to permeate your soul. It's impossible to be angry, upset, petty, or depressed when gratitude consumes you.

The second way to stay motivated is to focus on a compelling future. Steve Jobs, co-founder of a little company called Apple, once said, "Everything around you that you call life was made up by people that were no smarter than you and you can change it, you can influence it, you can build your own things that other people can use. Once you learn that, you'll never be the same again."[1] You are smart enough to accomplish anything that human beings have accomplished so far and, perhaps, even things that humans believe impossible.

College is designed to teach you how to shape the world. Whether or not you learn how is up to you. Some students go through college whining and complaining about every little thing and doing the absolute minimum to pass their classes. Then they struggle later in life and go around saying things like, "College isn't really necessary. Just go to a trade school and make money." On the other hand are the students who understand the value of college and want to learn how to shape the world. They are profoundly grateful for this opportunity. They study hard yet efficiently. They read and research and always do more than what's expected of them. And at the end of their programs, they emerge as knowledgeable, understanding, skilled, and capable people who will spend their lifetimes contributing to society and serving others.

That's your compelling future. You're capable of anything, and college can give you the knowledge, context, connections, mindset, social intelligence, and skills necessary to help you build a new and better world. So determine to fill your college years learning and doing new and noble things. Sometimes plowing through a mountain of accounting homework or learning the archaic names of all the tendons in the human body won't feel noble and grand, but it is. At such times you will need to fill yourself with gratitude and remind yourself of the compelling future that will be yours because you know how to balance a financial statement or repair an athlete's tendon.

College really isn't about doing well on tests. It's about learning to be a whole person. The sooner you grasp this concept and make it work for you, the sooner you'll become a great student, and being a great student who learns to be a whole person is far more important than getting A's. Besides, by focusing all your energies on becoming a whole, highly educated human being, you'll find that the A's come a lot easier.

The greatest secret is to link your gratitude to your compelling future and awaken your true motivation. As a result, you'll love college and develop a lifelong, insatiable desire for knowledge, which will carry you to most meaningful form of success—a life abundantly lived.

Chapter One

Using the Spacing Effect to Study Less and Learn More

[The spacing effect is] one of the most remarkable phenomena to emerge from laboratory research on learning.

—*Frank N. Dempster*

Many students struggle because they work against the way their brains want to learn. They believe learning is a simple equation: time spent studying = knowledge acquired. It's certainly true that *no* studying will equal *no* learning, but the best path to retaining knowledge involves more than following a simple formula.

To understand exactly how we learn, we need to know how our brains record information. When we learn something for the first time, our brains record that information in neurons. At the same time, the brain files the new information with related information by building connections between neurons.

The problem is that our brains can't imprint new information firmly enough in our neurons during the first exposure for perfect retention. The brain stores the information and establishes connections with related neurons, but the first impression is weak. Apparently our brains don't take kindly to strangers.

We know this instinctively, so we study harder, spending hours at a time reading information or doing example problems over and over in hopes that the information will sink into our maddeningly inhospitable neural structures. Immediate repetition does help, but our brains can only strengthen connections so much in one sitting, even if we go over the information repeatedly.

No matter how much time you spend cramming the day before a test, or even two or three days before a test, the connections you've made won't have had enough time to strengthen, and you may do badly.

Stop fighting your brain. If your brain doesn't want to remember stuff it has been exposed to for only a short amount of time, stop pressuring it. You'll waste your time and energy on the impossible.

As with anything that we don't like about reality, we can either whine and do nothing to help ourselves or we can figure out how to use the situation to our advantage. And it's easy to take advantage of reality once we understand something called *the spacing effect.*

Psychologist Frank N. Dempster calls the spacing effect, "[O]ne of the most remarkable phenomena to emerge from laboratory research on learning."[1] He has good reason to say this. Those who used the spacing effect in laboratory experiments on learning did significantly better than anyone else when trying to recall what they had learned.

Hermann Ebbinghaus, who conducted many of the early experiments on the spacing effect, first described it in 1885. Ebbinghaus noticed that retention increased when a person spaced the time spent studying information instead of shoving it into one time slot (a.k.a. cramming). Those who reviewed the information at *spaced intervals* remembered it better and for a much longer period of time.

Researchers have since discovered that the number of spaced exposures to information, not the amount of time spent with said information, is what really counts. Reading through your notes once per day for a week, for a total study time of one hour, leads to better results than going over your notes fourteen times in one day for a total study time of two hours. Multiple exposures are important, but even more so is the time in between exposures, which allows your brain to develop strong connections.

You can study fewer hours per week while learning more if you work with your brain rather than against it. This technique alone—once I learned how to apply it—completely transformed my college life. It's the most important technique I describe in this book.

If you adopt the spacing effect alone for your own study plan, your college life will become a lot easier. But when you use the other success principles in conjunction with the spacing effect, you'll notice dramatic leaps in your learning.

How to Jump-start the Spacing Effect

Applying the spacing effect is easy. It just takes practice to figure out what works best for you.

The theory says that the more spaced exposures you get, the better. How many is ideal? I recommend at least eight to ten spaced exposures, leaving several hours to several days between each of them. To achieve this goal, start racking up repetitions immediately. The easiest way to do this is to read the assigned readings before class, go to the lecture, and then review your lecture notes before going to bed. You'll get three spaced exposures while most of your classmates get one: the lecture (unless they're sleeping, texting, or committing other academic sins).

Before using spaced exposures to reinforce information, you must get that information in your head. This is why it's vital to read assigned chapters and other readings at least one day before a lecture. Reading will give you an overview of the concepts you need to learn and a first exposure to all the important details.

Listening to the lecture and taking good notes reinforces what you read and develops more neural connections. At night, when you review your lecture notes, you get a third spaced exposure. Some top students need only these three steps in order to succeed: they never have to study the information again. I always needed more steps, but if this works for you, rejoice. For those of us who lack genius, it's a little harder—but not much.

When the Test Looms

As the test approaches, the spacing effect becomes a lifesaver.

Let's say that a midterm is seven days away. How can you use the spacing effect to conquer that exam? First, it's crucial that you start reviewing for that exam today. You've already had three spaced exposures by reading, attending lecture, and reviewing your notes, but you'll need *at least* five to seven new spaced exposures to everything that could show up on the exam in order to master the material. Doing five spaced repetitions was always adequate for me, but seven was the ideal number. You won't know how many are ideal for you until you experiment. Just be sure to leave several hours or a full day between each exposure so your brain can cement those neural connections before you add another repetition.

Getting five exposures in one week might sound impossible. Don't worry; it's really not. In the next section of this book, I'll describe how to effectively review an entire textbook chapter in less than ten minutes. Using surveying, you can review all chapters, notes, and readings in about twenty to thirty minutes per day (of course, this depends on the reading load. But the higher the reading load, the more time you will save using surveying over traditional review). If you get five to seven spaced exposures at twenty to thirty minutes each, you have reviewed for only an hour and forty minutes to three hours and thirty minutes for an exam. Not bad.

After a week of spaced exposures, you make it to test day. You have followed all my recommendations. Each week, you read the assigned chapter(s) the day before the lecture. You went to lectures and took Pulitzer Prize-worthy notes (just kidding—please don't work that hard). On the evening following each lecture, you reviewed the notes you took that day. Then, a week before the test, you started reviewing all assigned readings and your lecture notes once per day. Perhaps something happened and you missed a day or two, but that's okay because you were shooting for a minimum of five spaced exposures.

By following these steps, you exposed yourself to everything that could appear on the test a total of eight to ten times. Most of your classmates came nowhere near this number of spaced exposures, which are vital for strong retention. Best of all, because you used surveying, you have studied less than most of your classmates, yet you are very likely to get a solid A.

Top Students in Their Own Words: Lisa, PhD, Psychology: University of California, Riverside

Jonathan: Thanks again for telling me about the spacing effect. Nothing has had a more profound effect on my college life. You're to blame for all my success and I couldn't be more grateful.

Lisa: Thank you very much. I'm just so happy when I hear that my teaching makes a difference.

Jonathan: How did you learn about the spacing effect, and how did you apply it to your studies?

Lisa: I learned about it in a cognitive psychology class that I took as an undergraduate. I began studying for each of my classes once a day, rather than the night before a test, and it changed everything for me. I studied for less time but got way more out of it. This also allowed me to identify what was confusing so that I could get clarification before tests.

Jonathan: Did you use any other study techniques?

Lisa: The only other technique I used is that I would re-write all of my notes from class right before a test. That really helped to jog my memory for what was important. I used the same techniques in all classes.

Jonathan: As a professor, what are some things that make you impressed with a student? What student behaviors irritate you?

Lisa: I'm impressed when a student shows up to class on time and prepared (meaning they have read the chapter before it is discussed in class), comes to office hours with questions prepared (written down), and relates class material to real life.

I'm not sure what is most irritating, but I'm surprised when a student rarely attends class, does not complete homework assignments, and does poorly on tests, and then emails me two weeks before the semester is over asking for extra credit because he or she needs an A. Those types of situations are difficult to respond to.

Jonathan: Anything else that you feel helped you be a good student?

Lisa: Probably the critical ingredient to being a good student is the *desire* to be one!

* * *

Crib Notes

You'll be getting a lot of information in this book, so multiple reviews will be important when you're working to incorporate the techniques into your daily study system. After you're finished reading, and you're doing spaced repetitions, you can hit the Crib Notes sections for a refresher. You can find a complete list of all Crib Notes sections in the back of the book.

1. Space study time to allow the brain to create and develop effective connections. Allow several hours to several days between repetitions, though one day is usually optimal.
2. To get the maximum number of exposures, read assigned chapters before class, attend lectures, and read your lecture notes before going to bed. These three steps will start the spacing effect process.
3. Prepare for exams by reviewing all test materials, such as textbook chapters and lecture notes, once a day for a minimum of five days. Don't "study"—simply read through everything once. Five to seven exposures got me an A on difficult tests. Experiment to find your ideal number.

Chapter Two

Use Surveying to Review Textbook Chapters in Ten Minutes or Less

I sat in an upstairs classroom lit with buzzy fluorescent lights. Posters of obscure books and English grammar charts were tacked to the walls. Across from me sat a short, pallid, overweight married man with two young children at home. He bragged about cheating on his wife and how he'd bought a house and two cars and maxed out his credit cards with the intention of declaring bankruptcy. He was loud, rude, and disrespectful.

At the next table sat a tall, thin black man who worked the night shift at a grocery store. He was humorous and positive—the life of the class despite his constant lack of sleep. Beside me sat a young Latina woman with braces. She was always happy to discuss her boyfriend problems with me, and they were numerous and fascinating. Bankruptcy guy would eye her hungrily when she wasn't looking.

A twenty-one-year-old Hispanic man sat on my other side. He kept me rapt with stories of the race wars that raged in his high school. He had scars from participating in the brawls. He wanted to be an airplane mechanic, but he wasn't doing well in his classes and would probably never see the inside of a hangar.

Our professor, a middle-aged woman with short, conservative hair, had pleasant features yanked down by a permanent frown, no doubt the result of years spent dealing with the reluctant students who filled the community college in which I sat.

This was a college reading course, the easiest class I had ever taken. But about half the students were failing. They complained about work and time constraints and then bragged about parties attended, movies watched, and beach sessions enjoyed.

Here in the midst of my discomfort and boredom, I learned one of the best study techniques in existence—one that, in a heavily modified version, has saved me countless hours of study time. It was called the SQ3R textbook reading method.

Surveying: A Better Way to Review Chapters

SQ3R had a certain academic sex appeal for me. It consisted of logical steps, and it used all kinds of complex techniques devised by lofty researchers. How could something so complex and well thought-out not work?

Despite sounding good, the technique was so yucky and time-consuming that no one in the class used it. Basically, it's safe to ignore any technique that's too complicated. With tweaking and combining it with the spacing effect, however, SQ3R goes from complex and unpleasant to simple and effective. I call the tweaked version *surveying.*

The first step in surveying is to read an assigned chapter in its entirety—preferably the day before the class in which it will be discussed. Reading a chapter in its entirety will make a thorough first impression on your inhospitable neurons. Don't worry about highlighting or writing any notes: Read quickly and take it all in. (If time is short, you can even skip the actual reading. More on this later.)

When you're ready to review the chapter, it's time to survey. By "survey," I mean a quick pass through the chapter that doesn't involve reading every word. When you survey, you concentrate only on the crucial stuff. Surveying after reading might sound counterintuitive; many students are naturally inclined to survey *before* reading a chapter. But if you first read the chapter in its entirety, afterward you can review all the most important ideas in that chapter in about five to ten minutes. This will let you review all the chapters covered on a test in just a few minutes a day, allowing you to rack up many spaced exposures while spending little time studying. The combination of the spacing effect and surveying is the real secret behind getting fantastic grades with little effort.

For a survey to really hit all a chapter has to offer, you must know exactly what to pay attention to. When surveying a chapter, read all titles, boxed items, photo captions, vocabulary definitions, graphs, bulleted points, any bolded or italicized text, any other text that is emphasized and, most importantly, the first sentence in every paragraph, finishing with the chapter summary.

Reading the first sentence in each paragraph is essential, because the first sentence is usually the topic sentence (notice how the topic sentence of this paragraph contains the vital idea, while what follows elaborates on that main idea). If the first sentence is not the topic sentence, keep reading until you find the topic sentence, but know that it almost always comes first or second. If the first sentence isn't the topic sentence, make a mark at the beginning of the sentence, such as an X, so you'll know to skip it when doing your spaced reviews. When you do find the topic sentence, underline the first word or otherwise mark it so you'll know that's the one to read when surveying. If you come across another sentence that you can't help but mark, underline the first word or make some other small mark to remind yourself to review it. But don't get carried away and mark everything as vital for review.

The topic sentence gives you the gist of the entire paragraph. The following sentences are there to support and expand on that topic. By reading all emphasized text and the first sentence in each paragraph, you'll get the main points, which are likely to make up the test, and you'll be reminded of the details in those paragraphs. To see how this works, pick up any textbook and read the topic sentence in every paragraph. You will find that 90% of paragraphs start with the topic sentence and that, by reading these and all other emphasized text, you can get a basic idea of what those pages are trying to teach you.

To finish the survey, read the chapter summary. The summary neatly ties up all the main ideas in the chapter.

And there you have it. That's surveying—simple, but oh so deliciously powerful.

It can be tempting to never read an entire chapter again. Why not just survey and get all the main ideas that way? Sadly, those windy supporting sentences often give great context for remembering information, and you should read them. You can do well if you use only surveys, but you'll find that the best results come from reading the whole chapter first and then using surveys for review. If you don't have time to read a whole chapter, however, using surveys alone will teach you most of what you need to know in a fraction of the usual time.

Another exception I always granted myself when I was in school was this: If I had a textbook that was really awful—one that I physically couldn't read for more than three minutes or my brain would go zombie apocalypse—then I just used surveys. Life is too precious and too short to waste on unnecessarily difficult reading. If the reading is extremely tedious, there's a good chance that no one else will absorb the whole chapter anyway. You'll be way ahead of everyone by simply memorizing the main points.

How to Combine Surveying and The Spacing Effect

After much trial and error, this is the method that I devised for integrating surveying and the spacing effect into my study system.

First, I read an assigned chapter in its entirety the day before class. I read quickly, almost never taking time to highlight or take notes, since almost all the important stuff in textbooks is bolded, italicized, charted, found in the topic sentence, or otherwise marked. If I wrote anything down, it was questions for the professor.

On class day I would go to the lecture, take good notes, and review those notes before going to bed, giving myself three spaced exposures to the information. Afterward, I wouldn't worry about reviewing the material until a quiz or test approached. At this point, surveying became invaluable.

I would start reviewing five to seven days before a test. I used surveys to review chapters, hitting all the most important ideas in the chapter in minutes. Reading the first sentence of each paragraph reminded me of its main idea and supporting material, and the chapter summary neatly tied up the overarching ideas. If I didn't remember what came after a topic sentence, I dipped into the paragraph until I recalled exactly what the author was talking about. I ended my review sessions by quickly reading my lecture notes. Thus, I would review everything that would appear on a test in a few minutes a day, giving the spacing effect enough repetitions so it could work its magic. It's all about reinforcing the initially learned information at spaced intervals.

This combination of surveying and the spacing effect can save you hours of study time while still allowing you to memorize everything you'll need to know for exams.

Stop Using Selective Reading

One common study technique is selective reading. Students innately understand that it's impossible to read everything multiple times before a test. Thus, they try to guess what the professor finds most important and then read only those sections of the textbook.

This is bad.

Selective reading, while it can save you time, almost guarantees that you will lose at least half a letter grade on exams. Professors will choose questions from all sections of the textbook, whether you read them or not. This isn't the end of the world if those questions are multiple choice or true and false. But what if you find yourself facing an essay question from the unknown? It happens. Now you're terrified about your grade and you're back to stressing. Stressing is not okay for a great student, and that's what you are now.

Stop using selective reading. Read everything once, if you can, and then use surveys to memorize all the key ideas.

Crib Notes

1. Read a textbook chapter in its entirety.

2. Do spaced chapter reviews, or surveys, by reading only titles, boxes, graphs, and photo captions; bulleted, italicized, or underlined text; and the topic sentence in each paragraph (usually the first sentence: if not, mark the topic sentence on your initial reading so you can find it later). Finish by reading the chapter summary. Finally, read your lecture notes.
3. Enjoy the hours this technique can save you.

Chapter Three

How to Crush Math, Double Your Reading Speed, Take Notes, and Own English

How to use English and the Spacing Effect to Conquer Math

Does the mere thought of doing math make you want to curl into the fetal position and sob yourself into a coma? For you math wizards out there, know that this is exactly how facing math feels to everyone else. There's a good reason why: your brain is actually hurting.

Research from the University of Chicago has found that, for those who have math anxiety, the anticipation of having to do math lights up the same areas of the brain that respond to pain. Your brain can't tell the difference between having to do math and burning your hand on a stove.[1] So if grabbing a hot stove sounds more appealing than factoring, please know that you're perfectly normal.

No fewer than fifty-seven times throughout my college career would I have happily burned myself in order to forego math. When I took the math placement test at my local community college, I placed into remedial algebra 1. No surprises there. I took the class and failed. The professor was bad, so I blamed her for my failure. I barely passed on my second attempt and went straight to hell—err … algebra 2.

Algebra 2 is a foreign language, one that I imagine few innately understand and even fewer know how to teach. I failed my first attempt. Again I blamed the professor. I registered under another professor for my second attempt, but on the first day of class the same professor walked in.

After two weeks I gave up. On my third attempt, I managed to pass—barely.

Determined to avoid college algebra, I registered for an intro to statistics class, which fulfills the college-level math requirement for a management degree. I failed the class by two points.

After failing stats I transferred to La Sierra University, a liberal arts school in Riverside, California, with an awesome business program (our Enactus team, formerly known as SIFE, is the only team in history to win back-to-back World Cup titles, beating the Ivy League schools as well as hundreds of other universities around the world). To my horror, remedial classes such as algebra didn't transfer. I had to take La Sierra's math entrance exam. I placed back in algebra 2, where I failed once again.

Finally, on my *fourth* time taking algebra 2, I scored. The professor understood that not all of us have an innate understanding of math. He fixed this problem by giving us English-brained learners instructions that we could understand.

Each morning he went directly to the board and wrote a list of the exact steps necessary to solve whatever new problem we were going to learn that day. He started with the first step, writing exact instructions in English, and then moved on to step two, and so forth, until the entire problem was represented in concise, easy-to-understand sentences. He would then work a couple of examples, referring to the written instructions to illustrate how they translated into that horrible language of letters, lines, and numbers. I was in heaven, or at least purgatory (I was still in a math class).

I started doing better immediately. It was also around this time that I learned about the spacing effect, so I tried something new. Instead of spending hours doing examples to try to memorize how the problems worked, I started using the spacing effect to memorize the English instructions. Each day I would go through my math notebook and read the step-by-step instructions. Soon, through the power of the spacing effect, I had each step memorized. When I went into exams, I knew exactly what to do because the instructions were right there in my memory. I got an A in the class, the first A I had ever earned in math.

The takeaway is this: If you and math don't mix, treat your brain to English instructions and then use the spacing effect to commit those instructions to memory.

But what if your professor is part of the 99.9999% of math professors who don't understand your insatiable hunger for common-sense instruction? I'm sorry. You'll have to write your own. Write the steps down as best as you can during class, and then piece them together more fully by using your textbook. It would be nice if textbooks had a concise, step-by-step instruction list for each type of problem, but their English directions are often interlaced with examples that use the haunted scribblings of Satan—err … numbers and symbols.

Putting It All Together

In time I refined my process. Not only would I write each step in English, but I would also write an example of the problem and each of its variations. Each type of math problem has slight variations that can trip you up on an exam, so be sure to write out an example of each variation for studying with spaced reviews. Now when you do your spaced reviews you can read through the steps and look at the example problems, and you're done! Easy.

If you still want more help with math, consider using tutors at your school (usually free) or turn to YouTube. YouTube is filled with helpful souls who often explain problems better than your professors. Better yet, you control their little puppet strings. Didn't catch something? Pull their strings, rewind them, and listen again.

If normal folk on YouTube don't cut it, go to www.khanacademy.org, where a former hedge fund analyst named Salman Khan will happily explain anything from 1 + 1 to vector calculus. His website, now backed by some big shot named Bill Gates, can teach you economics, chemistry, astronomy, finance, and many other disciplines. The website also has courses that help you prep for many standardized tests. All of this is free and fantastically done.

Crib Notes

1. Write down all steps for a math problem in English. Be specific, covering every step.
2. Write down an example problem and each possible variation. Include enough examples to make sure you can translate the English instructions into actual math.
3. When prepping for a test, review those written instructions and the selected examples daily until you have them memorized. Remember, it's not the amount of time spent studying that counts: it's the number of spaced exposures. Don't "study": just read over everything once per day.
4. Still need help? Turn to the Internet. Use YouTube, www.khanacademy.org, and everything else on there that can help you. Just remember that you can't use the Internet on the test.

Double Your Reading Speed: How to Eliminate Vocalization and Push Your Sub-Vocalizing Voice to the Limit

"The only way to do all the things you'd like to do is to read."

—*Tom Clancy*

"I cannot remember the books I've read any more than the meals I have eaten; even so, they have made me."

—*Ralph Waldo Emerson*

A great student needs strong reading skills.

The act of reading is simply taking information in through your eyes and storing it in your brain. Many speed-reading programs promise to increase your reading speed to thousands of words per minute, allowing you to breeze through books and remember everything you've read. After spending time and money on such programs, I can tell you that they didn't work for me.

Reading speed can usually be doubled, but that's about it. Most people read about two hundred to four hundred words per minute. This is roughly the speed at which people can speak. A strong reader, however, can read about eight hundred words per minute.

Most people are stuck at two hundred to four hundred words because they vocalize while they read: they move their tongues and throats, or actually mouth words. Even if they don't make any sound, this silent vocalization limits their reading speed to the speed at which they can vocalize.

If you want to increase your reading speed, eliminate vocalization. Focus on your tongue, lips, and throat, and make sure they aren't trying to articulate the words as you read. If you have trouble keeping them still, place your fingers on the offending areas.

Sub-vocalization, which manifests itself as the voice in your head that pronounces the words as you read silently, also holds people back. Many speed-reading programs claim to eliminate this voice so you can read at über, hypersonic light speed!!!

Maybe this works for some people, but the voice in my head lawyered up and successfully fought against eviction. Also, if I try to read without the voice in my head, I don't remember a thing.

But you can kick the voice in your head into high gear. Once you eliminate vocalization, you can push your sub-vocalization voice to great speed. Be warned, however, that your sub-vocalizer is lazy and has been sleeping on the job for a long time. It will take effort to beat him into shape.

To practice increasing your sub-vocalizing speed, pick up some light reading that has no impact on your grades. Try to read one of your favorite novels as fast as you can. Push your sub-vocalizer to the point at which you can still understand what's happening, but just barely. Soon, after practicing reading as fast as you can, your normal reading speed will begin to increase. Keep practicing and you'll eventually make it up to around eight hundred words per minute. This will feel fast. Your sub-vocalizer will be talking a lot faster than normal people do, but soon the speed will feel like second nature. This will save you countless hours in college.

You don't have to do anything special to increase your reading comprehension. Reading faster increases comprehension: When reading fast, you can more easily remember what was at the top of the page by the time you reach the bottom because less time has passed. This allows you to easily connect ideas and concepts, while slow readers forget things by the time they come to the next idea. Keep pushing your sub-vocalizer to faster rates, and better comprehension will follow.

Reading more will also lead to better comprehension. Constantly learning new words and phrases will help you become more comfortable with the written word in general. You'll start reading faster, which leads to greater comprehension. Reading is like any skill. More quality practice means better results.

Crib Notes

1. To increase reading speed, eliminate vocalization. Make sure that your lips, tongue, and throat aren't trying to pronounce words as you read. Any vocalization limits your reading speed to the speed at which you can speak.
2. Push the voice in your head to read at a faster rate. By constantly pushing this voice, your comfortable reading speed will eventually increase to about eight hundred words per minute or more. Reading faster also increases comprehension, as you will link ideas together before you can forget them.

How to Take Notes

Taking notes can be an enormous waste of time or, if done well, can help you bring home top grades.

Don't waste time taking notes on what you should already know. Many students don't read assigned chapters before class. Thus, when the professor starts talking, everything she says sounds new and important, and such students scramble to write it all down. This is the worst way to take notes, because these students are spending most of the class only half-listening to the lecture while frantically trying to transcribe it.

By reading the assigned chapters the day before a lecture, you'll know what the book covers and you won't need to write down those facts and concepts. This gives you more time to focus on what the professor says, which then gives you a better second spaced exposure to the information.

Having read your chapters, you'll also know when the professor says something new or better explains an idea from the book. Capture what she says with a brief written summary. In addition to being quick and easy to read later, this constant summarizing of key ideas is gym time for your brain. By constantly grasping ideas and bending them into your own words, your brain remembers those ideas well.

Also, during the lecture, write down questions that arise so you can ask your professor about them after class. Be sure to leave a little bit of space in your notes to write the answer once you get it.

Lots of students have fallen into the habit of taking notes on their computers. Don't follow their example. While typing on a computer seems faster, multiple studies have shown that students who write by hand remember information better. There's something about the act of writing by hand that links your brain to the ideas you're writing down.

The computer will also seduce you into writing too many notes, copying most of the lecture verbatim. This robs you of the useful exercise of summarizing ideas in your own words and gives you a lot more reading to do when you review the notes later. Finally, a physical notepad won't allow you to check Facebook if you get bored.

Don't Take Notes While Reading

I recommend not taking notes while reading a textbook. Some students like to take notes and create their own summaries of textbook chapters, but I always preferred to use surveying and the spacing effect to memorize the content and save my note-taking for the lecture.

If you write down anything while reading the textbook, write questions for the professor and ask them in class or afterward. Not only will this help you get your questions answered, but you'll also win thousands of good-student points from the professor for caring to read the chapters before class and thinking up questions about them.

The only time I would write notes while reading was for science textbooks. We'll talk about this soon, but for now, just worry about getting thorough first exposures.

How to Review Notes

Since I banned you from using a computer and you've only written notes that complement your readings, you probably won't have that many notes to review. Rejoice in a manner that doesn't conflict with the guidelines in your student handbook, and then get down to actually reviewing the notes.

Reviewing notes is easy. Fold the notes into your study time as you review assigned readings with the surveying technique. Use surveying to get a spaced exposure to the chapter, and then read through the notes of the accompanying lecture. As with the chapter reviews, read through the notes only once a day for seven to five days before the test, trusting the spacing effect to help you memorize them.

Crib Notes

1. Read all assigned chapters and readings before the lecture. Now you can take notes only on what outside materials don't cover, freeing up your time to really listen to the lecture.
2. Don't write down notes while reading your textbook. If you write anything, write down questions for your professor.
3. Review notes when surveying related chapters.

Writing Killer Prose: How to Quickly Master Writing by Practicing Osmosis, Seeking Out Quality Feedback, and Committing Outright Plagiarism (But Don't Plagiarize Your Papers)

Two of the most valuable things a student can learn for college, and for life, are reading and writing quickly and well. Being a strong writer will help you dominate college and, beyond college, you'll write proposals, emails, reports, memos, grad school applications, and more. Some people manage to forge through life writing badly, but that's a steep uphill battle that you don't want or need to fight.

Classes like composition will help improve your writing, but great students recognize that strong writing is a priceless asset and that it's wise to spend extra time mastering this skill.

Four Hacks for Mastering English

There are four simple ways to master writing. First, read more. Reading good prose will automatically help your writing by exposing you to everything the written language can do.

Second, pay attention in English class and study your textbook. Your professor and your textbook will teach you all the rules for proper English.

Third, get great feedback. Your professor should provide great feedback on your work, but sometimes this isn't enough. Your campus probably has a writing center where helpful souls like English graduate students will look over your work and help you through some of the language's gnarliest thickets. Spend time in the writing center.

Fourth, copy magazine articles by hand. If your writing needs serious help ASAP, start copying magazine articles by hand into a notebook. Some of the best writers in the world write for *Time, The New Yorker, National Geographic, Popular Science, Wired, Popular Mechanics,* and other top-circulating magazines. These writers are masters of conveying massive amounts of information effectively using beautiful, sensual language. Copying their articles by hand will force you to slow down and notice spelling, grammar, punctuation, word use, paragraph structure, and all the other technical ins and outs of the written word. You'll also get a strong sense for how to write effective essays. Most magazine articles are essays. Various articles inform, persuade, argue, and do the other things you'll be required to do in your essays. You'll see how good writers quickly introduce a topic, bring in outside research, support their arguments, and summarize their work.

A professor of mine who emigrated from Lebanon used this technique to learn written English. He would spend half an hour a day copying his textbooks by hand. He now has a PhD in marketing—no small feat for a non-native English speaker.

I used this technique for several months when I started college. My writing was horrible and I needed to quickly improve it. I probably spent around ten to fifteen minutes a day copying by hand from bestselling novels until I felt comfortable with the language. I learned so much so quickly that I can't recommend this technique enough. A friend later told me that copying magazine articles worked better for her because of how similar they are to essays. So perhaps you'll get more benefit from magazine articles, but I believe copying any great English by hand will help you.

Top Students in Their Own Words: Brian, PhD in Religion: Baylor University

Jonathan: What did you do to get such great grades, both at Duke University for your master's degree and at Baylor for your PhD?

Brian: I would go through my books once and highlight and underline all the most important stuff. Then, I'd copy what I had marked to my notebook, basically creating a condensed version of each chapter. To study, I'd just read through my notebook. Actually, I hardly studied at all. After spending so much time creating the outlines by hand I usually had a pretty good grasp of all the material.

Jonathan: Any other advice for how to study?

Brian: Be fascinated with the subject. Cultivate a deep interest in it. Always go to class with a great attitude.

Jonathan: What if you hate your major?

Brian: Change it as quickly as possible.

Jonathan: I imagine you wrote lots of papers to earn a PhD. Do you have any advice for writing papers?

Brian: For papers, it's all about coming up with the right questions. Ask the questions and you'll find the right paper topic. You don't want to be too broad or too narrow. And whatever you do, don't just recount facts. Think and engage with the material in an original way. Original thinking and application is what makes a great paper. Think about when in the paper to introduce your own voice.

Great papers must also be tailored to the professor, as he or she will be the one grading it. Figure the professor out—kind of a sad reality but a true reality. Of course, read the instructions carefully and follow them. Many students seem unable or unwilling to follow directions.

Finally, don't be afraid to ask the professor about the paper. Tell them you want to write a good paper and then follow whatever advice they give you. If you say you want to write a great paper, they tell you what they want in a great paper, and then you produce what they asked for, they can't give you a bad grade, right?

Jonathan: Anything else you wish to share?

Brian: You can never know what you're thinking until you write it down. Use a journal to keep track of your thoughts about certain topics. This is really important for writing papers. Don't just think about a paper—

start putting stuff down. Only by writing can you create complete thoughts. Normal thinking just leads to partial thoughts.

* * *

Tips and Tricks

A simple way to impress your professor is to vary your sentence length. If most of your sentences end up close to the same length, your writing will feel boring and stilted. Shake it up. Write some long sentences, some short ones, and some complex ones. Your professor likely won't notice why he likes your writing so much, but he'll sense that it's mature and interesting. The secret is the sentences. Keep them varied. Keep them interesting. You won't always be able to control your sentences on your first draft, but when you're revising your work, be sure to take a look at your sentence length. You can always break up long ones or combine related thoughts into compound sentences.

Use small words. No matter what you're trying to convey, count on small, everyday words to do the heavy lifting. Like ants, small words can carry many more times their weight, especially when they work together. Thus, "commence" becomes "start." "Magnanimous" becomes "selfless." You're welcome to use the colorful and subtle nature of larger words now and then, but don't rely on big words to sound smart. Smart people worry only about getting the message across.

Use small sentences. Even though you want to vary your sentence length, lean mostly on short, declarative sentences. A few writers are masters at writing long, complex, beautiful sentences that are easy to follow, but if this isn't your strength, focus on keeping sentences short and to the point (that's about as long a sentence as I can get away with).

Make an effort to write in the active voice. Format your sentences like this: subject, verb, rest of sentence. Instead of writing, "The dog was walked by Ted," write, "Ted walked the dog." See what happened there? All I did was place the subject of the sentence, "Ted," at the beginning. Suddenly, the sentence makes more sense because it's in a proper order of subject, verb, rest of sentence. We can also drop the word "was," making the sentence cleaner. Let's try that again: "The study was conducted by five researchers from Harvard" becomes "Five researchers from Harvard conducted the study." Here's another: "The milkshake was being made by Korman" becomes "Korman was making the milkshake." If you want to learn more about writing in an active or passive voice, go on Google and search for "how to write in the active voice," and you will find guides that go into much more detail.

Good writing sounds natural. It resembles what you'd say in real life. You wouldn't call a friend and say, "At this point in time we should schedule a meeting in the dining commons." You'd say, "Let's do lunch." A commitment to sounding like a normal person will ensure that your writing is clear and understood.

Finally, write things of value. Don't just turn in papers. Turn in works of value that you wrestled with. Most students can wing a five-page paper on a given subject and end up with a half-decent grade. But your professor can tell when you're winging it, and your paper will bore her. Put in the effort to create something special. Your professor will notice and you'll get in the habit of caring about and being proud of your work—something that will become extremely important when you're in the working world. Perhaps your professor will give you a passing grade on a throwaway paper, but your future boss will smell a half-baked, steaming pile of valueless malarkey from ten miles away.

Please don't look to this book as an example of proper college writing. I've written this book in a conversational style that's inappropriate for academic writing.

Crib Notes

1. To master writing, read more. Exposing your brain to all a language can do will improve your spelling, grammar, and vocabulary.
2. Carefully study your English textbook and pay attention in class to learn the rules of proper English.

3. Take advantage of your campus's writing center to get feedback on your writing.
4. If you need to take drastic measures, copy magazine articles by hand into a notebook.
5. Vary your sentence length to keep your writing interesting.
6. Use small words and small sentences, and write in the active voice.
7. Make sure your writing sounds similar to speech, but more polished.
8. Don't just puke ink onto pages. Value your work and put your best efforts into creating something you're proud to turn in.

Chapter Four

Unleash Boundless Creativity and Build a Knowledge Base

Turbocharged Creativity: Flexing Your Subconscious Muscles to More Easily Write Papers, Do Projects, and Make Presentations

To preserve your sanity, you'll need a strategy for dealing with big papers, projects, and presentations that require lots of writing.

Big assignments require your brain to do a lot of work. You have two options: you can toil ceaselessly and force your brain to grind out page after page, or you can give your subconscious permission to do it for you. The latter is much easier.

Your subconscious loves to do work for you. But your subconscious is like a lazy employee a few weeks from retirement: You can't force it to work any faster than it wants to.

The easiest way to get on the good side of your subconscious is to give it plenty of time to work. For the big assignments that require lots of writing, schedule time blocks in your planner to work on them. If you have an eight-page paper due on a Friday and you think it will take three hours to write it, divide those three hours into various work times scheduled throughout a couple of weeks.

You have probably experienced working hard on a paper and then running out of ideas. You left the paper for a few hours and did other things. When you returned to your work, more ideas magically appeared in your brain. That's your subconscious slowly but dutifully working for you.

To encourage this process, your subconscious needs you to return regularly to your paper and work on it a little bit at a time. Each time you work on the paper, your mind comes up with questions about how it will proceed. You can try to force yourself to think of all the answers in one sitting, or you can simply ask yourself the question, "I wonder what should come next?" and then go do something else. Even though your conscious mind won't be thinking about it, your subconscious will get right to work. All it needs is a problem to work on and time in which to solve it.

You'll find it helpful to schedule a block of time both in the morning and in the evening to work on projects or papers. When you work on a project in the morning and come back in the evening, your brain is ready to expand in different directions and integrate new information. Your papers will be easier to write when you don't have to dream up all eight pages in one or two sittings. Often, you'll have to write only a paragraph or two at a time—an easy task. Soon you'll finish your paper and it will feel like you exerted little effort. This process might even free up time to do a revision or two or five, which is sure to raise your final grade.

If you're like me, you'll tempt fate and go without a day planner in which to record due dates and schedule study times. Like me, you'll get into trouble now and then when you realize a big paper is due tomorrow and you haven't written a word. I recommend being smarter than I am and carrying a day planner. Many great students do so and it saves them a lot of trouble.

Another way to harness your subconscious power is to start working on a big project the moment it's assigned. You don't have to do much right away—only enough to get your subconscious curious. Once you've hooked your subconscious, you can relax until a couple of weeks before the project is due.

You can hook your subconscious by immediately reading the project prompt a couple of times, making sure that you understand exactly what the professor wants. If anything is unclear, or you simply want some tips, go to the professor, tell her that you want to get an early start on the project, and ask for ideas (and win about 448 good student points).

Then, take a moment to write down your initial thoughts about the paper. Perhaps you can sketch a partial outline, or maybe the introduction. Scour your mind for anything you've read recently that you feel would be a good source. Write it down along with anything else you think might end up in the paper.

These few minutes of effort are critical. You're handing your subconscious a to-do list, its favorite gift. It now has something to mull over, and it will faithfully get to work.

You'll start to notice your subconscious working almost immediately. While sitting in a different class, you'll hear the professor say something that would fit perfectly into your paper. Since you're an unstoppably great student, you whip out your pen and write it down. A newspaper article mentions a piece of research that would support your argument perfectly; you snap a picture with your smartphone and email it to yourself.

By familiarizing yourself with the project and doing a little bit of work right at the beginning, your subconscious is now on high alert for information that will help it write a great paper. Keep this up for a few weeks and, when you sit down to actually write, you'll have tons of ideas and sources all ready to go. The paper will practically write itself.

This is why great students are able to efficiently write their papers. They are constantly picking up ideas, arguments, and sources while going about their lives. They've harnessed the power of the subconscious mind. Now you can, too.

Crib Notes

1. For big papers and projects, give your subconscious permission to do the work for you. Instead of forcing your brain to come up with all the pages in one sitting, work on your paper for only a few minutes per day far ahead of the due date. Your subconscious will use the extra time to search for answers, new directions, and new associations to bring into the paper.
2. Spend a few minutes working on a project as soon as it's assigned. Read the prompt several times, write down any ideas that come to

you, and try to write a partial outline or introduction. Now that your subconscious knows what needs to be in the paper, it will search for ideas and sources in other classes and readings.

Building a Knowledge Base

"A person who won't read has no advantage over one who can't read."
—*Author unknown*

Imagine a car engine. Its complex machinery has nearly been completed, but it's missing the timing belt. If you take the belt and put it on the engine, suddenly the engine is fully connected and able to sustain internal combustion.

Now, take the belt off the engine, lay it on a table by itself, and carefully watch to see what happens. You'll be shocked to see that ... nothing happens.

Sadly, our minds work in the same way. In order to learn something new, we must connect what we're learning to previous knowledge we have gained through experience or reading. Without making such connections, the new knowledge is as useless as a belt lying by itself on a table and will eventually fade from our minds.

This leads us to one of the most profound and undervalued study techniques: building a knowledge base. This is vital because the more you know, the more you can learn.

Many of the most admired people in politics, business, science, and the arts are living (or dead) examples of how powerful this study technique can be. Warren Buffet, who at the moment is the third-richest man in the world, is said to have read all the books on finance and investing held at his local library by the time he was twelve. As a child, Nikola Tesla read the entirety of his father's immense library. Benjamin Franklin read every book he could get his hands on when he was young. Abraham Lincoln reportedly read so much that his father beat him for neglecting his farm chores. "Abe read all the books he could lay his hands on," said his stepmother. "And when he came across a passage that struck him he would write it down . . . then he would re- write it—look at it—repeat it."[1]

Before arriving at Harvard, some students read the Harvard Classics. Charles Eliot, president of Harvard University from 1869 to 1909, was challenged to put together a collection of the best works of world literature. After a year of work, he'd gathered and edited an anthology of fifty-one books, each of which are 400 to 450 pages in length. Eliot felt that one could gain a liberal education by reading from these selected works each day.

Let's say that each book in the Harvard Classics anthology comes to 400 pages. This means that students who read this anthology arrive at Harvard having read 20,400 pages of what's considered some of the best literature in the world, not to mention all the other books, journals, magazines, blogs, and other publications such a student has probably read.

Most people haven't read fifty-one books in their entire lives.

Such deep and varied reading lays a killer foundation for succeeding in college. Students with this background start college with a massive intellectual engine that covers enormous swathes of human history. They know about war, peace, science, art, manufacturing. They've lived hundreds of lives through the eyes of kings, slaves, soldiers, and every other type of person in human society, hopefully giving them an understanding and empathy for people of all races and social strata.

When students like this sit in a chemistry class, they aren't just struggling to understand the chemical reactions they are learning about. They're remembering how the study of chemistry led to the purification of saltpeter, leading to gunpowder, and the incredible effects that invention still has on society. All these connections they're making to previous knowledge allow them to connect the belt of chemistry with their intellectual engine. The missing link of chemistry knowledge pops into place and they *get* chemistry.

Another student, one who hasn't taken the time to develop a strong knowledge base, struggles with chemistry because he has little context with which to connect this new knowledge. It's like placing an engine belt onto a table by itself. It merely lies there, disconnected from anything meaningful. This is the kind of student you'll hear whining about how impractical chemistry is and how it won't relate to anything he will do in life. Such statements (especially about math) show that a person has no understanding of how important such disciplines are to our modern world, which depends on science and technology.

Building connections to a knowledge base goes back to the spacing effect. Before entering their classes, avid readers have usually run across the ideas and terminology that will be used in their classes multiple times. Being exposed to the information in class deepens and expands the knowledge they already have, giving them new spaced exposures.

To average students, avid readers seem something akin to learning gods. It's easy to think that they have brilliant recall, but really they only have a deeper and wider knowledge base. When such students read their class textbooks or sit through lectures, they attach meaning to what they are learning by placing the learned information into the theoretical frameworks they have developed in their knowledge base. Thus, the time they spend learning is more efficient than it is for students who haven't read much.

So what can you do to start building a knowledge base? Reading the Harvard Classics wouldn't hurt, but a lot has changed since 1909 (for instance, the Harvard Classics anthology includes almost nothing written by women). So what should you read?

Everything.

Start with what interests you. Read a book about it. Then read a book about something you know nothing about. Read a book about history. Read five books about history. Look on the Internet for lists of the best books ever written. Read some of them. You'll discover things you've never heard about that completely fascinate you. Chase those veins of interest and learn about them. Over time, you'll find yourself growing an enormous knowledge base. And then, when you're sitting in class, you'll be amazed at how what you are learning connects to history and to a multitude of other disciplines.

So start reading. You'll develop a massive framework of knowledge that makes learning new things easier. You'll find your classes fascinating and you'll learn faster than the students around you who haven't read as much.

Don't have time to read? Nonsense. Read in the bathroom. Carry a book in your backpack and read instead of aimlessly checking your phone every two minutes. Install the Kindle app on your phone. Read on some of your breaks at work. You don't have to shirk society in order to become a better reader. Simply take advantage of those small gaps in your day and soon you'll surprise yourself by the amount you have read and how that reading is helping you with your education.

Crib Notes

1. The more you know, the more you can learn. The mind hangs new information on the knowledge frameworks it already possesses, so the more knowledge you have, the easier it is for your brain to make associations with new information. Thus, read deeply and widely to gain as much knowledge as possible.

Reading for Sources

Think of your brain as a high-turnover library. As ideas come in, they are sorted and placed on elegant, modern shelves. But little stays in the library for long. Within a couple of weeks, ideas vanish into the hard-to-reach expanse of your long-term memory. If your library of ideas hasn't been updated recently, it's difficult to come up with a lot of great ideas and sources when you sit to write a paper.

One way to keep your head filled with great ideas and ready-to-use sources is to regularly read good books, newspapers, and high-quality publications.

Most great students are voracious readers. They read everything they can get their hands on. When I was in college, I averaged thirty extra-curricular books a year. I also read an article or two per day from the *New York Times*. I read *The New Yorker*, *Popular Mechanics*, and *National Geographic*. My Internet reading included Science Daily (a website that puts the newest science research into understandable language) and a variety of conservative and liberal political blogs. I also listened to a number of podcasts and audiobooks in the car.

I don't say all this to brag. Besides providing fun, this reading contributed to my success as a student because I had a large knowledge base on how the adult world works, and I had well-developed opinions on a variety of topics. And, since I started working on papers the day they were assigned, I was constantly finding information to include in my papers and presentations. By becoming a well-informed, well-rounded citizen, I was essentially writing my papers all the time.

A big part of writing papers is having something to say. Great students develop strong opinions on myriad topics. To form a good opinion, you'll need to know a fair amount about a subject. The more you read a spectrum of high-quality books, magazines, and newspapers, the more opinions you'll develop about all kinds of issues. It's also important to realize that these are the books and publications your professors are reading. If you are as current and informed as they are, you will stand out.

When you do this, the term "research" doesn't mean "a mad scramble to learn something about the topic." It's usually a brush-up on the issues at hand and a search for the perfect supporting, academic sources.

Tactfully presenting well-formulated evidence or value-based opinions founded on careful reading and thought, combined with the righteous passion that burns within when you believe you're right, will help you appear intelligent and thoughtful.

In addition to your textbooks, it's good to read bestselling, mainstream books on your major topic. Often, such books will be a lot more fun to read and will give you context on which to hang the theoretical knowledge you learn from your textbooks and classes.

Coming from a business background, a lot of my non-assigned reading focused on materials that would contribute to my classes. If you're in other fields, feel free to tailor your reading accordingly. For instance, if you're a biology major, consider subscribing to biology publications or check them out of the library. These will keep you abreast of the latest ideas and research in the field, give you an expanded sense of where the principles you are learning can take you, and solidify your theoretical understanding of the field. You'll also be giving yourself spaced exposures to all kinds of jargon.

Crib Notes

1. Read a variety of high-quality books and publications. You'll develop well-rounded opinions that look great in papers, have tons of sources already identified for many topics, and develop a knowledge base that will help you learn new things at a fast rate. Also, papers are difficult to write only if you have nothing to say. Wide reading will give you plenty to say.

Chapter Five

The Art and Science of Science

Thinking God's Thoughts After Him

Johannes Kepler once described the process of science as "Thinking God's thoughts after him."

Sometimes it feels as though one needs a god-sized brain to wrap one's head around science. And sadly, there are no huge hacks for helping you learn science. But with the right mindset and a few tips, science goes from nebulous and scary to manageable.

As we talked about in the introduction, the best students are those who have a desire and determination to learn. They perceive the value of what they're learning and thus come to love the learning process. Perhaps the greatest way to get excited about learning science is to consider its value and majesty. Science is the study of matter, whether it's alive or inanimate, energy or antimatter. If anything matters in this life, it's matter.

Matter, its interactions, and all the beautiful things composed of it (consider yourself exhibit A), is so complex that we will never figure it all out. Yet in the pursuit of this impossible goal we come face to face with the grandest mysteries the human mind can attempt to understand. To work in this space is a privilege that will add intellectual richness to your life.

Before taking a geology class, you will drive by a mountain and think, "Huh, big mountain." But after a geology class, you'll drive by it and think about how tectonic forces shoved that big mountain out of the earth's crust, how its granite formed through volcanic forces far below the earth's surface, and how erosion created the alluvial fans that spread out from the ends of its gorges.

The same goes for biology, chemistry, astronomy, and any other science you may choose to take. The world becomes infinitely more fascinating once you understand some of the machinery that makes it tick.

So, the next time you're solving some long chemistry formula, try to see it as a sliver of the majesty of understanding the universe you are blessed to inhabit.

The Spacing Effect for Science

Science requires tons of memorization. As we learned earlier, the spacing effect is the best way to cram information into the inhospitable expanse of our long-term memory. Unfortunately, science textbooks don't usually lend themselves to review using the surveying method that works so well for other disciplines, which makes getting spaced repetitions difficult. What's more, most science problems rely on math, making them harder to grasp and remember than ideas.

Faced with these complications, I recommend a hybrid approach with the techniques we've learned so far. First, read your assigned chapters in their entirety before class, except this time keep a pencil or highlighter in hand. Science textbooks are usually far denser than other textbooks and reading only the topic sentences for spaced surveys won't be enough to remind you of the ideas in the rest of the paragraph. Thus, when you run across a formula, definition, fact, or particularly important sentence, mark it for later review. Don't bother highlighting the whole thing. Just underline the first word or something. In this way you should eliminate the need to go over the context that you now understand but that you can safely skip during future reviews.

After reading and marking up your chapter, go to your lecture and take careful notes. Review those notes before going to bed.

You've now had three spaced reviews to all the information you'll need to know. Not bad. But you'll probably find that with science you'll need many more spaced reviews in order to memorize all the facts, formulas, lists, and so on. So, after doing these three steps, take a new section of your notebook, title it, "Stuff I Have to Know in Chapters X-Y," and then write down everything you need to know from your textbook, lecture notes, and homework.

For example, from my geology textbook I would write, "Muscovite is a type of mica that has one direction of cleavage, producing thin sheets. It's related to two other forms of mica, biotite and chlorite, and its chemical formula is KAI2 (AISi…." Then I would write down a couple of questions from the homework that asked about muscovite, and then list the correct answers. Thus, I took everything I needed to know about muscovite and reduced it to a few sentences.

After doing this for each chapter, I'd have a running cheat sheet of everything I needed to know for the class. By creating these cheat sheets, I gained a fourth spaced exposure, which was a high-quality exposure because it involved summarizing and writing everything by hand. Then I could read through my "Stuff I Have to Know" sections once per day until, through the power of the spacing effect, I had everything memorized. This usually took me seven to ten spaced exposures, especially for the gnarly stuff like formulas.

Even though this is a lot of work, ending up with a single condensed list of the critical information to use in spaced reviews will save a lot of time over wading through the textbook and solving example problems.

For problems that require a lot of math, you might find it helpful to create step-by-step English instructions for how to solve the problems and include a couple of examples to show how those instructions translate into the numbers. Thus, when you're reviewing, you won't have to do lots of examples—you'll simply have to memorize the instructions and their translations.

Associations and Mnemonics

Associations help us remember things by linking new information to knowledge we already possess. For instance, if you're trying to remember how many vertebrae humans have in each section of spine, remember, "We have breakfast at seven, lunch at twelve, and dinner at five."

Mnemonics can also help you remember the names and orders of lists. Here's a common mnemonic for the first ten elements in the periodic table: "Happy Henry Likes Beer But Could Not Obtain Four Nuts." The first letters of the words in this sentence correspond with Hydrogen, Helium, Lithium, Beryllium, Boron, Carbon, Nitrogen, Oxygen, Fluorine, and Neon.

Add mnemonics to your notebook and review them frequently so the spacing effect can help you memorize both the mnemonic and the list. Remember, it's inefficient to repeat information over and over many times in one day in an effort to memorize it, for the brain can only build neural connections so strong in one day. With a list or a mnemonic, repeat it a couple of times and then move on to something else. Review it again hours later or the next day.

If it helps to create your own mnemonics and associations, then go for it. Otherwise, there are tons of clever mnemonics only a Google search away.

Top Students in Their Own Words: Steven, Bachelor's in Biology from California State University East Bay

Jonathan: What techniques did you use to excel in the sciences?

Steven: In high school I learned about *memory castles*, also known as *Roman rooms*, which worked really well for me. So when I got to college, I started using them to remember formulas, definitions, data sets and everything else I needed to know for the sciences. But I also found that they worked equally well for remembering information in my non-science classes.

Jonathan: What's a memory castle?

Steven: A memory castle is a visual world for the things you want to remember. Let's say you're learning chemical formulas. You could try to remember that information by repeating it over and over again, or you could create a memory castle to help tie that information to visualizations.

When I make a memory castle, I use a very familiar location such as my house. In my imagination, I walk into my house and look at everything that's inside. If I'm trying to remember something specific, like a formula, I'll associate it with something in the house. For instance, I'd walk into my memory castle, take a painting off the wall, and write the formula on the back. Later, when I want to recall that formula, I'll go through the whole process again: walk in the front door, go to the painting, take it down, flip it over, and read the formula.

Jonathan: Would you remember that formula after one association? Or would you need to do it multiple times?

Steven: For complex information I might have to associate it several times, repeating the process of walking inside, taking down the painting, and writing down the information. For simple things, it usually takes me only one association.

Don't be afraid to get a little crazy with this idea. Maybe you're trying to learn the territories taken over by Genghis Khan. Walk into your memory castle, open up a bedroom door, and have Chewbacca jumping on the bed, screaming out the names of each territory. The more unique the visualization the easier it can be to remember it.

Jonathan: Any other tips for memory castles?

Steven: Create a different memory castle for each subject you're studying. Or even each class. I keep the same memory castle of my house, but I will have many copies, each with a different colored front door. So, if I need to remember something for my anthropology class, I'll walk into my memory castle with the red door and start making associations, even if those same objects have associations in a different memory castle.

Jonathan: Any thoughts on study routines?

Steven: I found that the better prepared I was to study, the more efficient my study time became. For instance, if I'd been drinking, eating terribly, or avoiding exercise for any length of time, I had a terrible time learning new information. So while I was in school, and especially when I was within a few weeks of big exams, I made a huge effort to eat healthy, get plenty of exercise, and avoid drinking.

When I sat down to study, I shut out all distractions except for music. I'd play stuff I knew really well—songs that could fade into the background. Songs without lyrics. Yo-Yo Ma playing Bach's cello suites or the Goat Rodeo Sessions. I liked electronic music too.

Jonathan: What was your experience with Adderall?

Steven: I was prescribed Adderall for my ADHD, and I was pleasantly surprised to see how much it improved my focus while studying. But even though I could focus, my retention got much worse. For instance, while building my memory castles, the information I associated with objects just wouldn't stick as well and I'd have to use many more repetitions. Also, if I studied on Adderall but wasn't on Adderall when I took the test, I seemed to be in a different mental state and had even more trouble accessing what I had studied.

Adderall works by increasing neurotransmitter activity, and I suspect that one of the side effects include altering the way the brain stores information, leading to worse recall. But that's just my suspicion. In any case, I went off my Adderall when I really needed to study.

* * *

Crib Notes

1. Learning science will greatly increase your intellectual enjoyment in life, not to mention give you the skills to exist in our technologically advanced society. Learn to love science.

2. Science requires memorizing details, so lean heavily on the spacing effect. Read assigned chapters before class, marking anything that seems important. Go to class and take good notes, and then review those notes before going to bed. Later, create a cheat sheet in your notebook and record everything you suspect you'll need to know for tests, such as facts, formulas, questions from the homework, and more. Review this cheat sheet daily until the spacing effect helps you memorize all the important details.
3. Learn to use associations and mnemonics to help you remember complex lists and number sets.

Chapter Six

Taking Tests: Tips from Beyond the Realm of Preparation

The Test

You've done everything right. You've pre-read your assignments. You've attended every lecture and taken award-winning notes. You've gone to bed early, eaten healthy, and exercised often. You've reviewed your notes and chapters for several days using surveys and have taken full advantage of the spacing effect.

And now The Destroyer rises from your professor's mind and haunts a stack of papers. This amalgamation of evil and murdered trees becomes what's known as an exam—the gnarliest opponent most of us will face in college. I just got shivers … well, not really.

But tests can be frightening. Make no mistake: Test anxiety is a real condition.

I come, however, bearing good tidings. Exams are toothless paper tigers if you follow the example of great students. For them, taking a big exam is no real cause for anxiety. This may sound absurd, but it's true. What's their secret?

Their secret is preparation.

I know such a profound statement is likely to blow you away, but please try to contain yourself.

In truth, great students have more than one secret, but 95% of crushing a major exam is preparation. By doing everything right, as I've described in earlier chapters, you ought to be fully prepared for any exam. If today is exam day and you aren't ready to absolutely own that exam, then you didn't get enough spaced exposures to the information. It's almost as simple as that.

I've talked about skipping that six-hour panicky review the day before an exam and instead cutting that review in half and redistributing those hours throughout the semester. By pre-reading your assignments, taking careful notes, reviewing those notes before going to bed, and then using surveys and the spacing effect, you have been studying all along for the exam—only in a much more effective way.

But on top of all this, great students still have a 5%-trick up their sleeves

The Other 5%

Top students complement their preparation with great test-taking skills. First are pre-test rituals that get rid of anxiety. Of course, the best medicine for text anxiety is thorough preparation. There's no reassurance like having all the material basically memorized. Bless the spacing effect ...

But it's also helpful to keep reminding yourself that, unless this is some pivotal test that decides whether or not you go to med school, or whether or not your parents cut off financial support, your grade really doesn't matter that much. Even if you crash and burn in catastrophic fashion and get an F-, you'll still be okay. Life will go on and you will survive. You'll have plenty of time throughout the class and throughout the rest of your time in college to make up for it. Even if it is the MCAT you're dreading, you can always take it again, and you've got other options: you've always liked playing the saxophone ... So take a deep breath and determine to laugh and go out for pizza if you get an F. And trust me, if you follow the techniques I've been describing, you will not get an F.

First, get plenty of sleep before the exam. Nothing will screw up mind and body like pulling an all-nighter, or even a half-nighter. Remember, if you have to stay up late studying the night before the exam, you're shattering about nine of the ten great student commandments. Something went wrong a long time ago.

Studying right before the exam is a sure way to awaken anxiety. Don't do it. Wake up, do a quick review if you must, and then do something relaxing, preferably an activity that involves movement. Go for a walk around campus. Go to the gym and get sweaty. Enjoy a long, relaxing, healthy meal with friends.

As the exam approaches, make sure you leave enough time to get to the classroom early. Once you're in place, do something fun until the moment the exam starts. Don't review anything unless you absolutely have to. If you don't know it by now, you aren't going to learn it in five tense minutes. All you'll do is work yourself up and hurt your chances to effectively use the information and skills you *do* know. Read a novel, play a game on your phone, flirt with someone.

Since my brother and I shared many classes, we often played Hacky Sack while waiting for an exam to start. Outdated, maybe; geeky, yes, but it put us in a good mood before the test and other students would often join in the fun. Don't underestimate how important it is to be in a good mood before a test.

During the Test

The test has started. You are prepared, relaxed, and in a good mood. Now what?

The first thing you must do is read every question before you answer anything. This assumes, of course, that you have lots of time to take the test. Sometimes you won't have that luxury, but if you do, take advantage of it.

This is important for a number of reasons. First, reading all the questions wakes that lazy foreman in charge of your subconscious. In the Turbocharged Creativity section, I talked about how the subconscious mind works for us at all times: all it needs is some information and a problem to solve and it will get right to work. That's exactly the process you want to jump-start during the test.

You may have had the experience of walking out of a test and suddenly realizing that you wrote the wrong answer for some of the questions. This happens because your subconscious has just gotten around to dredging up the necessary info. Feed your subconscious the questions first so that it can help you during the exam. This technique is especially helpful for essay questions. Your mind can work on compiling everything you know about that particular question while you work through the rest of the test. Then, when you return to the essay prompt, your mind will hopefully have generated some interesting things to say.

Finally, surveying the questions lets you begin with the easiest ones. Unfortunately and fortunately, our brains are easy to trick. By answering the easiest questions first, the brain limbers up and releases all kinds of chemicals that relax us and get us in the "I got this" mood. The "I got this" mood is far more constructive than the "I'm going to fail and my parents are going to cut me off and I won't be accepted to med school and my girlfriend is going to break up with me" mood.

Negotiators use this same principle. They try to get their opponents to say the word "yes," even if it's to irrelevant questions. If opponents have said yes five times, they are more likely to say yes when it really counts. Same for tests: The more questions your brain gets right, the more questions it will continue to get right. Let your brain get used to victory. While your victorious brain is breezing through the easiest questions, your subconscious is taking advantage of the time to process the hardest ones.

One note of caution: If you know that the test will be tight on time and you feel confident about crushing the exam, you probably shouldn't read *all* the questions first. It can take a few minutes to read the exam, and if taking those few minutes guarantees that you won't have time to answer questions, then it may not be worth it. In this case it may be better to quickly skim the test, noticing what kinds of questions are being asked and where the highest-point questions lurk.

Once you become confident in your test-taking abilities, you won't need to read all the questions first. When I got used to using all these study techniques, I would feel so prepared and confident before tests that I never read the tests beforehand. I answered the questions as they came and rarely got the wrong answer on more than a couple of questions.

If You Can't Think of the Answer Quickly, Skip the Question

Many students bomb timed tests by trying to answer every single question in order. They run into a hard question and, not knowing the answer off the tops of their heads, struggle for two minutes searching their brains for it.

If you don't know the answer almost immediately, there's little chance that it will surface in the next few minutes, if ever. Those few minutes are better spent moving on. It's better to skip a few one-point questions in order to answer a few ten-point questions. Leave a mark beside the question you're struggling with. If you have time, you can always come back to it. After forty-five minutes, your mind may have remembered the answer.

Never Second-Guess Multiple Choice Questions

Studies have shown that our first impressions of simple questions are usually correct. If you finish the test with time to spare, do not change any multiple choice, true or false, or fill-in-the-blank answers.

If you second-guess yourself, you'll usually pick the wrong answer the second time around.

Recheck Formulas, Data, and Essay Answers

If you're blessed with extra time, it's smart to return to any math, data entry, or essay questions.

It's easy to screw up formulas or data entry. One tiny mistake at the beginning can throw off the rest of the problem. Often, going back to these questions will reveal such a blunder.

For essays, go back and read the prompt to see if you failed to answer or fully elaborate on one of the sub-questions. If you find you did miss something, write an extra paragraph and draw an arrow to where it should be inserted. Content is king, and most professors won't mind the arrows.

Essay Questions

An essay prompt usually brings up a main issue and asks several mini-questions. Your professor expects intelligent discourse on that main issue and a response to each of these mini-questions. Many students, after a brief look, simply launch into the essay, get enamored with a tangent, and fill the allotted space. They feel great about their essays because they wrote a bunch of pretty words and cleared the word limit. When they get their grades and are docked for failing to answer everything the question asked, they're shocked.

Instead of writing essays that way, create a simple outline that answers each sub-question. These answers will become the topic sentences for each paragraph of your essay.

Then all you have to do is write an introduction and a paragraph addressing each sub-question, and you'll have a neatly arranged and thorough essay answer.

Still Having Trouble?

If you have learned and followed all these techniques and you still regularly experience test anxiety that hurts your performance, there might be deeper issues involved. Visit your school's counseling center. Its counselors will most likely be able to help you identify and work through such issues.

Crib Notes

1. Preparation is 95% of the battle. If you are thoroughly prepared, the test will not be an issue. Use the spacing effect and surveys to get at least eight to ten spaced exposures to everything that could be on a test.

2. Once in a test, read all questions before answering anything. Let your subconscious get to work. This is especially important for essay questions. Trust your preparation and skip this step if time is limited.
3. Answer the easiest questions first. This puts you in a relaxed mood, giving your mind permission to work at peak performance.
4. Don't get hung up on one question. If the answer doesn't come quickly, it probably won't come at all. Put a mark beside the question. If you have extra time later, come back to it.
5. Don't second-guess multiple choice or true or false questions. Your first impression is usually the right one.
6. Do recheck data entry questions, formulas, and essay answers. Often a tiny mistake in data entry or formulas will throw off the whole problem. Essays can always be expanded or tightened.

Chapter Seven

Small College Hacks That Make a Big Difference

Maximize Your Study Time: Why You Should Run Away from Study Groups and Avoid Distractions

Study (verb): The act of texting, eating, and watching TV with an open textbook nearby.

– *Anonymous meme*

Students get crazy about their study routines. Blasting AC/DC, drinking nonfat caramel macchiatos, and sitting at the fourth table from the coffee house door all become requirements in the quest to getting anything done, as does having at least three friends around.

Great students, too, are crazy about their study time. But, unlike coffee shop students, they are more scientific in figuring out what really works. If you bother looking up the research on learning, you'll learn that multitasking kills learning. Having the TV on in the background, listening to music (with the possible exception of the classical genre), trying to keep track of a conversation—these all destroy retention. And I hate to say this, ladies, but it's even true for you, contrary to popular lore about your mega-multitasking ability. Think of multitasking as multidistracting.

If you want productive study time, find a quiet place and hit the books hard. Keep your courtship with your books as private as possible. This will help you focus and avoid distractions. Anything that takes you away from studying causes your mind to switch modes and reorient on something else.

Then it has to take the trouble to switch into study mode again. You'll have forgotten the string of ideas that you were following and will need to backtrack to find it. This all takes time. If you ban distractions and stay focused during scheduled study times, you'll have more time to wholeheartedly enjoy music, TV, or quality time with your friends later.

Study groups are an abomination to learning. In my experience, most study groups conduct their meetings thus: slowly they convene, open their books, order coffee, and make small talk for fifteen to twenty minutes. They glance at their textbooks from time to time, maybe even study a few problems or paragraphs—a few pages if they're lucky. Soon three hours have passed. Everyone feels as if they've put in a lot of study time, but in reality they haven't learned anything.

Avoid such study groups. If you find a motivated group of people who are 100% focused on helping one another learn, it might be worth your while. Anything less will drag you down. Sharing study time might be more fun than doing it alone, but failing your classes will make that fun fall flat.

One exception I made to this rule was homework groups for technical classes like accounting, finance, and other math and science courses that required lots of delicate work. There's nothing as frustrating as spending an hour creating a balance sheet only to discover that, because you forgot one detail, you messed up near the beginning and now the whole sheet is wrong and you must start over. A good study group can prevent this kind of problem. If you get together to work on such problems, you can use your collective experience to work through them faster. You might not learn quite as much as you would have had you figured out the problem by yourself, but it's better to spend fewer hours trying to figure out the homework and apply the hours you've gained to reviewing the completed, corrected examples that you figured out as a group.

A word of caution. Some top students feel that they must figure out these delicate types of problems all by themselves in order to really understand them. Personally, I preferred the group setting and spaced exposers to memorize how to do the problems, but feel free to try it both ways to see what works best for you.

Top Students in Their Own Words: Kristel, Master's Degree in Public Policy: Harvard University

Jonathan: What made you such a great student?

Kristel: I think what helped me the most was my curiosity. I am curious, and that is what motivates my learning. Having a goal for what you study is also beneficial—whether it be a professional goal or something related to what you believe and what kind of impact you seek to have through your studies and work. Also, I am not afraid of hard work. Studying may require some sacrifices and discipline, but the rewards make it entirely worthwhile.

Jonathan: Any advice about study routines?

Kristel: People have different ways of learning. I have definitely been more of an individual learner than a group learner. I tried study groups a few times, but found that these were very time-consuming and not very effective. One-on-one studying could work, but for me that was the maximum size of a good group. Another thing was that I hardly ever studied late at night. I don't think learning after 10:00 pm is very effective, so I would rather get a good night's sleep and start up again early in the morning.

Jonathan: How'd you write your papers?

Kristel: Paper-writing to me is about exploring a subject in depth and learning about a narrow subject matter of interest. I spent a great deal of time preparing before writing a paper. I never sat down and just started writing. I would read various sources to obtain an understanding of the subject matter and different views on it. I always took copious notes while doing this. Then, I had fun playing with titles for the paper quite early on to define its direction. When writing the paper, I would set aside long blocks of uninterrupted time so I could delve into the subject matter and go deeper and deeper into it. I do not believe in writing papers off the top of the mind or with many interruptions. To write a good paper, you have to engage deeply with the subject matter. You have to understand it. And like anything else, the results and experience are best when the subject is something you are truly interested in exploring.

Jonathan: Any specific techniques for other disciplines, such as science?

Kristel: Science was a different kettle of fish, perhaps because it was not the subject matter that interested me the most. Repetition was key here, and liaising with students who understood the subject matter better than I did. Instead of struggling for hours and hours with a question I did not understand, I would seek out advice from the classmates who understood it the best. Then, I made sure to do all the homework thoroughly and read the textbook, underlining and taking notes. I did not cram, but tried to work quite thoroughly throughout the quarter.

Jonathan: Did you try to eat well, sleep enough, and exercise regularly during school? If so, do you believe your lifestyle choices impacted your academic performance?

Kristel: Absolutely. This may be among the most important factors in having a good experience and a positive outcome in college. Eating well with the amount of food that is readily available can be a challenge, and requires conscious choices. It took me a while to learn that. Living on a college campus may also mean not getting enough exercise. Then it is a good idea to make conscious choices about what to eat and drink. Cutting down high-sugar foods and drinks is a good place to start. I tried to get enough sleep, knowing that I did not function well as a student without it. Getting enough exercise also involved a bit of a learning curve. I didn't get it right from day one, and recognizing how much that means early on is a huge advantage. The mind and body work together, and they work best when both are in shape. Eating right, getting enough sleep, and exercising has to be prioritized, and it took me some time to get that right.

Jonathan: Did you feel it was important to befriend professors or to be selective about which professors you took classes from? If so, how'd you go about doing this?

Kristel: Befriending professors is not a technique to attain something—to get better grades or to obtain a good standing. But given that professors are generally knowledgeable, thoughtful, engaged individuals, getting to know them and discuss issues of interest with them is one of the greatest privileges of a liberal arts education. This was certainly my experience. I had an advisor that helped me select the courses that were of interest. I would also spend quite a great deal of time shopping for classes. This is because I did not want to miss out on getting the best professors. Sitting in on the first class would give me an idea of whether this was a class and professor that would be of great interest. Once the class began, I did get to know some of my professors very well, working with them as a TA or discussing paper topics, and even discussing existential questions and matters of faith. It was a privilege, and is highly recommended.

* * *

No Bad Classes

Nothing ruins a semester like a bad class. Maybe you're not interested in the subject matter, or the professor should have picked a different calling, or the workload is unreasonably difficult.

When confronted with such a class, many students fire up their whining machines, dial their determination engines to eleven, and proceed to suffer through the rest of the semester. They feel there's some rite of passage inherent in sticking out bad classes and coming out on top.

Great students don't care about rites of passage. Whenever possible, before they even sign up they talk to students who have already taken the class so they can determine who is the best professor. They look the class up online and read reviews. They know their own strengths and weaknesses and work with their advisors to avoid classes that don't utilize their strengths.

You can't do algebra to save your life, but you need a college level math? Take statistics (I found it to offer an infinitely more useful skill set). You can't stand chemistry but you need a science class with a lab? Take geology or astronomy. Music and art appreciation surveys often cover fine arts requirements for those who dread the idea of actually having to sculpt something.

In high-level courses and those with complicated subjects, it becomes even more essential to find the great professors. Even organic chemistry or advanced calculus can be fascinating if you find a professor who gets unreasonably excited by tiny living things or extremely complex math.

Another way to filter classes is to sign up for more classes than you intend to take, attend the first day of each class and see if it's something you really want to take, and then drop the classes that don't interest you. Before trying this, however, make sure doing it won't impact your financial aid.

Oh, and one more thing—there's a big difference between hard and ridiculously hard. Sometimes you want hard classes that will teach you something vital. Avoid unnecessarily hard classes that aren't teaching you efficiently. For instance, I once took an anatomy class in which the professor deducted points if lines drawn from our descriptions to the pieces of anatomy weren't perfectly straight. She regularly took away points for other infractions that she invented on the spot. That's not the kind of hard you need to endure.

Hard was my freshman composition class at a community college. We started with thirty-two students. By the end, twenty-four had dropped out. The teacher was HARD. Our first papers were so covered in red ink it looked as if she'd soaked them in blood. But, after a semester of her drilling into us the fine points of grammar and structure, our papers were better. My final paper received an A, one of the hardest A's I have ever earned.

Yet, thanks to that hard teacher, I learned. Throughout the rest of college I never got lower than a B on any paper.

But struggling to learn a tough subject from a teacher who can't make that subject come alive—that's ridiculously hard. It's not worth it. Do everything you can to avoid such teachers and college will be a wonderful, intellectually stimulating experience.

Take Regular Study Breaks

Despite your best efforts, despite faithfully using the spacing effect and surveys and doing everything else right, sometimes college or life will still throw you for a loop. There might be times when you must study for many hours in one day. This isn't fun, but how can you make the best of it?

It's easy, thankfully, to trick your mind into thinking that studying this much is not that bad. The secret is to take a ten-minute break after every fifty minutes of studying.

For some reason most people, including yours truly, can't focus on one thing for much more than an hour at a time. After an hour of intense focus, the mind throws up its hands in frustration and begins looking for something else to do.

When faced with such a situation, you can either fight your natural impulses and power through your studies, or you can strategically give in to your brain's demands. Being a strategic pushover is the easiest way to make a long study session bearable and to get the most out of it.

So, after forty-five or fifty minutes, get up and get moving. Go for a quick walk around the block, do some calisthenics, pull weeds in the garden, hit on some cute person who happens to be walking by your dorm, or whatever. The point is that it's much easier to think, "I only have to study for fifty minutes" than "Only four more hours to go ..."

It's important that your ten-minute break involves something active or at least radically different than your homework. Taking a break from writing a paper so you can write an email won't work. Some quick exercise will awaken your body and mind. Something radically different will change your mental gears enough so that, when you return to studying, you'll feel refreshed and ready to focus again. You'll find that you will accomplish much more this way than you would have if you'd powered through.

Recently, I heard an interview with Arnold Schwarzenegger in which he talked about how when he's memorizing a script or working on something else that requires a lot of concentration, he works really hard for about forty-five minutes and then takes a fifteen minute break to play chess or do something active. For him, breaking the routine and doing something he loves for a few minutes refreshes his mind. When he comes back to work, he's ready to attack it with as much energy and mental vigor as he had at the beginning of the day. This helps him to work like a Terminator … I mean, a machine.

Love What You Do

"Develop interest in life as you see it—in people, things, literature, music. The world is so rich, simply throbbing with rich pleasures, beautiful souls, and interesting people."

—*Henry Miller*

Do what you love … Ah, such a common and annoying cliché.

Since I haven't yet figured out how to make a living mountain biking, playing with my dog, and reading novels, I've had to do things that I don't love to get by. Chances are you will too.

But through this process I have learned a great study technique: Love what you do.

Many students act as though most of what they are studying is excruciating. They look like they've flatlined in class. They whine about the homework, complain to the professor about this or that, and are quick to tell you how they can't wait for the class to end.

How terrible to dislike what you're doing.

The best way to fight this rotten attitude is to look for reasons to enjoy what you're doing, even if you don't foresee it being enjoyable. This sounds like another common and annoying cliché, but it works wonders.

Almost everything you study in college is a topic of critical importance to society—even if some people think otherwise. Someone might say that the humanities are useless. When asked to cut funding for humanities classes during World War II, Winston Churchill replied, "Then what are we fighting for?" If it weren't for the arts, our world would be a bleak, mechanical place. On the other hand, if it weren't for the sciences, we'd be living in the Stone Age, too busy hunting and farming to worry about learning how to play the cello or make movies.

For whatever classes you're taking, try to identify what critical importance the subject has on the world. Do your absolute best to become fascinated with the subject, and if you can't, act like you are. Your professor, tired of listless students, will notice and immediately take a liking to you, which never hurts your grade. And, because self-deception is easy, by pretending to become fascinated in a subject, you may actually become fascinated by it, making your studies rewarding and enjoyable.

If you can't bring yourself to like your situation in college, don't hesitate too long before changing your major. Millions of students have done so over the years and millions more will in the future. Changing your major is, however, a big deal, so make sure before jumping ship that you aren't jumping into frigid water. Spend time looking into other majors. Talk to people in the majors that interest you. Shadow people employed in careers that require those majors. Such a transition may be hard to make, but working for decades in a career that doesn't interest you will damage your life more than adjustments to your academics possibly could.

I majored in management. I didn't hate my classes (well, maybe accounting), but I didn't love them either. Six months before graduating, I realized that business was boring. It didn't light within me a fire to do big and bold things. But with six months left in my program, I decided to finish it. It wasn't as exciting as another major could have been, but I knew a business degree would be useful for the rest of my life. Indeed, it has been invaluable so far.

After graduating, I went back to school and took film classes in the evenings after work. For the first time, I couldn't wait to go to my classes and I loved every minute of them. Loving my classes so much also makes it effortless to get A's and has inspired me to pursue a Master of Fine Arts in screenwriting at the University of Southern California.

That's the difference choosing the right major can make. Be practical when you have to be, learn to love what you're doing if possible, and always do your best to end up in a situation where you actually will love what you're doing. Such a commitment will make college enjoyable and will make those A's easier to reel in.

Top Students in Their Own Words: Ingrid, MD, Board certified in Internal Medicine and Infectious Diseases: #2 in her graduating class at the Loma Linda University School of Medicine

Jonathan: What do you think made you such a great student?

Ingrid: A number of things, I suppose. I always slept well, ate well, exercised, and studied hard. I think those are all equally important.

Jonathan: When you say you "slept well," what does that mean exactly?

Ingrid: I always went to bed early, usually around 10:00 pm. Then I would wake up at 5:00 or 5:30 am and study early when everything was quiet. I never missed sleep to study because, if I didn't sleep, I felt like any study I did was completely wasted. You can't study well when you're tired.

Jonathan: Would you mind elaborating on "ate well and exercised"?

Ingrid: I tried to eat a balanced, nutritious diet. I avoided junk food like the plague. I rarely ate dessert. As for exercise, I tried to powerwalk or jog every day. I also went to the gym often.

Jonathan: When it was time to study, did you have any routines or techniques?

Ingrid: There were a couple of things that I think really helped. First, I would never study for more than fifty minutes at a time. Every forty-five or fifty minutes I would take a ten-minute break and go for a walk or do something active. Taking regular breaks made studying so much easier.

Repetition was also essential. I always studied everything multiple times. You just have to get it to sink in.

Finally, I tried to never worry about failure. Failure is not death. You'll go on. Having said that, I must admit that failure took on more importance in med school. If you failed to learn something, it could mean death for your future patients, so I took not failing seriously. But I still didn't worry.

Jonathan: Anything else?

Ingrid: I would pray daily that I would learn what I needed in order to be a good doctor. And I believe that God granted this wish. There have been many instances in which I have diagnosed a patient based on something I heard only once in medical school. So pray, because God is happy to help you learn everything you need to know.

* * *

Go to Class

Students who are struggling will often, for whatever reason, skip classes. This is hugely damaging. Professors sometimes only announce things in class, not to mention give surprise quizzes and calculate attendance points.

Determine that only hell or high water will keep you from being in class, front and center, every single period. Over my five years in college, I believe I missed less than a handful of classes.

Perhaps Mark Zuckerberg skipped a lot of classes, still did well, and started a hundred-gazillion dollar company called Facebook. You aren't Mark Zuckerberg. Go to every class. Don't skip. Pay attention, take awesome notes, and repeat. Your grades will thank you.

Crib Notes

1. To improve the quality of your study time, eliminate all distractions. Multitasking reduces your efficiency. Think of multitasking as multidistracting. Find a quiet place and focus.
2. Stay away from most study groups. Conducting conversations unrelated to the subject at hand makes you lose twice: you don't enjoy your conversation because you know you should be studying, and you don't get any studying done because you're talking too much.
3. Technical classes are the exception to the above rule. Classmates can help you solve complex formulas and data-heavy problems. Such help can save you hours in the homework phase, giving you more time to review.
4. Don't take any bad classes. Ask around, research online, and sign up for more classes than you will take (just make sure adding extra classes doesn't impact your financial aid). Drop any class that threatens to be a misery. If you have to take a hard class, seek out a professor who is irrationally in love with the topic and is great at spreading that love.
5. Take a ten-minute study break every fifty minutes and do something active. This is an easy way to trick your brain into thinking, "I don't have to study for three hours, just for fifty minutes."
6. Love what you do. Make an effort to become fascinated with every class you take. If your program is consistently dragging you down,

however, carefully consider changing your major. There's a major out there that will engage your mind so you'll love going to classes every day.

7. Don't skip class. Go to every class. Just do it. Your grades will thank you.

Chapter Eight

Use Sleep, Exercise, and Diet to Keep Your Head Clear (Literally), Get Straight A's, and Avoid the Freshman Fifteen

More than Academic Techniques

You're already on the path to becoming a great student. You have an academic study system that's saving you time and bringing home the grades.

But there's still a lot you can do to make college easier, increase your success rate, and have more fun in the process. Lifestyle is the best stone to use to kill all these birds.

Many students get into trouble when they enter college. Suddenly there's an all-you-can-eat cafeteria stuffed with greasy, fatty, sugary cocktails that seduce the tongue and settle on the waistline. The dorm is a hyper-efficient echo chamber that doesn't quiet down until 2:00 am and there's no one to tell you to go to bed anyway. Classes, homework, meetings, and events suck up all free time and leave you with a lethargic, sedentary four years. The pounds pack on, the muscles liquidate, the skin pales, and exhaustion builds. Sickness takes hold of your dilapidated body and makes life a mucus-filled misery. You miss classes and the work piles up. Your body feels as though it's aged thirty years, your brain as though Alzheimer's is around the corner.

But you don't have to go through college feeling terrible. Well-rounded students take care of their health so that they can get the most out of college. With a few tweaks to a busy schedule and a little bit of willpower, the college years can be some of the healthiest, best-feeling of life. Getting plenty of sleep, eating right, and staying fit during college can take a lot less time and effort than you might think.

Sleep

While many studies have shown that getting at least seven hours of sleep is crucial to earning good grades, it has been discovered that the time you go to bed could have more impact on your grades than the total amount of sleep you get.

Not all sleep is created equal. Research shows that the expression "early to bed, early to rise" might be more than an old wives' tale. The American Sleep Association recently published a study that found that, "Compared to those with the lowest academic performance, students with the highest performance had significantly earlier bedtimes and wake times."[1]

The link between bedtime and academic performance seems to be found in the production of melatonin. Melatonin, a hormone produced by the brain, has been linked to rapid eye movement (REM) sleep. REM is thought to be the most important stage of sleep, as it is the stage the body craves the most. A sleep-deprived body finally allowed to sleep will fall into REM almost immediately, a process that normally takes up to ninety minutes to achieve. REM sleep is thought to aid in properly storing information in long-term memory—and long-term memory is important for students.

Melatonin, unfortunately, keeps limited hours. Production of melatonin is highest before midnight and then begins to taper off. If you go to bed after midnight, your body doesn't have time to create much melatonin, which may be why students who go to bed early have significantly higher academic performance than students who go to bed late. Another requirement for proper melatonin production is adequate sunlight. So crawl out of your dorm room once in a while and get some sun.

It's recommended that for the best melatonin production you should go to bed between 9:00 and 10:00 pm. Most students hate this idea. Many have gotten used to going to bed much later than this and have grown accustomed to studying late at night. While you'll get some results when studying late, it might be better to study less and get that pre-midnight sleep so melatonin can work its magic and you'll actually remember what you studied.

When I first started college, I regularly stayed up past midnight, reading. After learning about the above information, I made it a goal to get to bed by 10:00 pm. I noticed that I learned much more efficiently. I also noticed that other students who didn't know this information struggled. Many times before big tests students would say that they'd stayed up all night studying. I had usually spent about thirty to forty-five minutes studying the previous evening, had gone to bed by 10:00 pm, and had woken up at 6:00 am and worked out for a few minutes the morning of the test. I always got A's, while the students who studied all night, logging many more study hours than I had, often failed or barely passed.

Don't try going to bed early for just a few nights to see if it makes a difference—it won't work. To really see the difference, you need to be consistent. If you're following the rest of the advice in this book, you'll be learning new information and reinforcing it on a daily basis. By consistently going to bed early, you'll properly store what you've learned. The successive accumulation of knowledge by using the spacing effect and sleeping properly will lead to the best results.

And let's be honest. Isn't getting a full night's sleep a lot more fun than cramming? Wouldn't you love to get all the sleep your body needs? Of all the whining and moaning I heard around campus as a student, fatigue was the most frequent complaint. You'll enjoy college more if you aren't always stumbling around like a zombie. Treat yourself to all the well-timed sleep your body wants. Your body will thank you and so will your GPA.

If you're a die-hard night owl and feel tempted to hurl this book across the room, please don't! All I can say is that following this advice worked for me. Even those with terrible sleeping habits can do well if they use all the other techniques in this book, but finding a productive sleep schedule will make a huge difference.

Exercise

It can be difficult to fit regular exercise into a college routine, but the payoff can be greater than the time spent sweating. Exercise helps your body and mind function better. It also has a strong effect on emotional stability. Many argue that exercise is one of the best things you can do for your quality of life. When asked how he stays productive, billionaire businessman Richard Branson said, "I work out." He credits exercise for giving him four extra hours of productivity every day.

Research has established a link between physical activity and academic performance. A recent review of the available literature concluded that exercise is extremely important for students, with phrases such as "[W]e found evidence of a significant longitudinal positive relationship between physical activity and academic performance."[2] In English, this means that exercise leads to better grades.

I attended a colloquium in which one of my exercise science professors told the story of what exercise did for one of her students. The student approached her on the first day of the Lifetime Fitness class and said, "I hate exercise and I'm pretty sure I'm going to hate this class." (FYI, don't say this to your professors). At the end of the course, the same student approached the professor and said, "I still hate exercise, but I have to tell you what happened. I am a slow learner, and before this class I would study for eight hours a day to get good grades. After starting to exercise regularly for your class, I now only have to study for four hours a day to get good grades. I'm going to keep exercising."

You don't have to wait for more studies to tell you what you already know. Exercise is good for you. Don't skip it.

Exercise doesn't have to take a lot of time. Set aside as little as thirty minutes a day, and then let nothing short of death or finals interrupt it. Alternate a day of cardiovascular exercise—a vigorous walk, jog, swim, or bicycle ride—with one of strength training. Starting an exercise regime may not feel good for the first couple of weeks, but after that, you'll begin to feel miserable if you miss a workout.

We Are What We Eat

Health is not everything, but without it, everything else is nothing.

—*Hans Diehl, founder of the Complete Health Improvement Project*

Most people want to be healthy and fit, especially in college, where potential love interests abound. People also just want to feel good. Feeling good makes it a lot easier to study and do all the other things a great student must do.

Perhaps the best way to feel good, be healthy, and stay fit in college is to eat the right kind of diet. And what is the right diet? Nobody knows.

If someone were to quantify the exact amount of ink spilled on the subject of diet, I imagine the number would be in the hundreds of thousands of gallons. Every year dozens of diet books are published, as are countless articles. Then there's the constant tongue-wagging: Dr. Oz saying this, Dr. Ornish saying that, Dr. Agatston saying something else that contradicts both Dr. Oz and Dr. Ornish.

If the supposed experts can't agree, how are we supposed to figure out what's best for our own health?

I won't pretend that I have the answer, but I've found something that has worked well for me and hopefully can help you, too. After reading *The China Study* by T. Colin Campbell and Thomas M. Campbell and watching a series called *The Total Health Solution* by John McDougall during my freshman year of college, I adopted a whole-foods, low-fat, plant-based diet.

As soon as I stopped eating dairy, oil, and highly processed foods (I have always been vegetarian, so giving up meat wasn't an issue), great things happened. I lost twenty-five pounds in two months without any additional exercise. My post-nasal drip, which had given me a sore throat for almost two years straight, cleared up within days. I could train harder and recover faster and had more energy than ever before. Other benefits included sharper thinking, the clearing of acne, and better sleep.

At first, I thought going vegan would mean giving up good food for twigs, seeds, and possibly an assortment of grasses. But I soon discovered that eating a whole-foods, vegan diet didn't have to bore me. For instance, for breakfast today I ate oatmeal with blueberries, banana, and walnuts. For lunch I had teriyakied chickpeas on brown rice with mango salsa. For dinner I ate pad Thai and used the leftover mango to make Thai mango sticky rice.

I have strictly maintained this diet for the past four years and have never regretted it. I eat all I want, choosing from a huge variety of delicious foods. I rarely get sick and have plenty of energy for hiking, biking, surfing, and running.

Our bodies are like skyscrapers of almost-magical complexity and engineering, and they are constantly rebuilding themselves. They're composed of hundreds of billions of cells, all of which need thousands of separate nutrients in order to thrive. What if you built a skyscraper from mud and sticks? How can your body thrive on Cheetos and mac and cheese?

Whole, unprocessed plant foods are packed with macronutrients such as complete proteins, carbohydrates, and fats, as well as minerals, vitamins, and thousands of phytonutrients. Sadly, a lot of what passes for food has been so adulterated that hardly any of these essential properties remain intact. Whole wheat, for example, is bursting with nutrition. But if you take that wheat and grind it into oblivion, scrape away all the fiber, and bleach it until it's white, you're left with a substance your body can hardly recognize. This "wheat" spikes your blood insulin levels and wreaks havoc in your body. The same goes for olive oil, an unnatural source of calories. Squeeze the liquid fat from thousands of olives, removing this liquid from the fiber, minerals, vitamins, and phytonutrients that used to bind it, and consume that concentrated nutrient all by itself? That makes no sense whatsoever.

Your body craves nutrition, not just calories. You can give your body tons of calories, but it will still burn with hunger because it's starving to death. Feed your body. Don't worry about calories. If you feed your body unprocessed complex carbs, such as potatoes, corn, whole grains, brown rice, beans, fruits, and lots of vegetables, including green leafy vegetables, you will give your body the nutrition it needs.

If you want to check out the scientific literature behind such a diet, I recommend watching the videos on www.nutritionfacts.org. The physician who founded the website creates short videos on almost a daily basis detailing the nutritional research on a plethora of health topics. For everything he says he shows the medical or nutritional journal from which it came and explains any complex jargon. His videos are often humorous, easy to understand, and informative. If you want a really detailed look into nutrition, check out his yearly nutrition roundup lectures, which are around an hour in length and which summarize dozens of nutritional studies.

Another great resource for information on a total vegetarian diet is the documentary *Forks Over Knives*, written and directed by Lee Fulkerson. *The Starch Solution* by John McDougall is worth reading as well. If you really want to go into the weeds of nutrition science, you may enjoy reading *The China Study* by T. Colin Campbell. If you'd like to try a whole-foods, total vegetarian diet, some of the best cookbooks available are the *Happy Herbivore* series by Lindsay Nixon.

If you want to make dietary changes in college, be sure to talk to your doctor. I am not a doctor or health professional and anything I say about diet cannot be taken as advice.

How Diet May Affect Your Grades (and Your Whole Body)

In 1959, the *American Journal of Medicine* ran a study that detailed what happens to blood after a person eats a single high-fat meal.

Normally, blood cells are flexible. They can bend in half and squeeze through the tiniest capillaries to bring oxygen and other nutrients to cells all over the body. Blood cells are also charged and will bounce off one another, helping blood flow smoothly throughout the body.

The *American Journal of Medicine* reports, however, that within an hour of eating *one* high-fat meal, blood cells begin to clump together and blood becomes sludgy. The blood cells are coated by fat, which causes them to become rigid. They also become unable to repel one another. This rigidity and sludginess prevents the blood from adequately carrying oxygen and nutrients to your cells. The study found that six hours after a high-fat meal, blood oxygen levels dropped up to 20% and blood stopped flowing completely in the smallest capillaries.[3]

You don't have to be a doctor to realize that a 20% reduction in blood oxygen content and a traffic jam in the smallest blood vessels is bad. Other studies have found that such sludginess may reduce brain function, interfere with lung efficiency, cause fatigue, and lead to other problems. In other words, lots of dietary fat slows down and jams up the whole system.

Look around your school's cafeteria. You'll see students stuffing themselves with eggs, bacon, and cream cheese for breakfast. For lunch, they'll devour pizza, deep-fried onion rings, salad dressing (most dressings are mainly oil, a.k.a. liquid fat), oily spaghetti sauce, and so on. For dinner, a similar assortment of high-fat foods might be followed by ice cream or pie for dessert.

That fat happily enters the blood stream, where it coats your blood cells, jams the capillaries, and reduces your body's ability to distribute oxygen and other nutrients. Your body then stores some of that circulating fat as body fat, contributing to the freshman fifteen or the sophomore twenty.

After a day of cramming their bodies full of fatty foods, students try to study, but brain function is reduced because the brain isn't getting enough oxygen. These students may also feel sleepy during class and have trouble focusing on anything except the desire to nap. Tiredness after a meal is often thought to be caused by blood being sucked to the stomach to digest food, but in reality it's probably sludgy, oxygen-poor blood born of high-fat foods.

The best way to ensure that your brain and body are working at full capacity may be to avoid high-fat foods. As you'll notice from the interviews with top students that are scattered throughout the book, many tried hard to eat a healthy diet while in school. They believe their diet helped them be top students and now, thanks to the *American Journal of Medicine,* we might know why.

Top Students in Their Own Words: Larry, PhD, Syro-Palestinian Archaeology: Harvard University. Fulbright Scholarship Recipient

Jonathan: You were quite an amazing student. What were your secrets?

Larry: There are a couple of things that I felt were really important. I always read my assignments before class and during lectures I took very good notes. I also wrote my own outlines for each chapter in my textbooks. A distraction-free study environment was really important. I couldn't stand studying around noise. I also had to have a space dedicated to study.

Jonathan: Did you use any specific study techniques?

Larry: For lists of facts I'd use mnemonics like acronyms to help me remember them all.

Jonathan: Did you befriend your professors?

Larry: I did. I talked to them often. Asked lots of questions. I became very close to many of them. I think, if I had any "secrets," that this would be one of them. I think getting to know my professors was one key to my success.

Jonathan: A test is coming up next week. What do you do?

Larry: Well, I studied constantly, but the day before the test I would sit down with all my notes and summaries and do a thorough review. I tried to get to sleep, but I would often stay up to 2:00 or 3:00 am studying.

Once in a while I would study all night, even though I knew that wasn't good.

Jonathan: Did you try to eat healthy and get regular exercise and, if you did, do you think it helped your academic performance?

Larry: I never worried about those things.

Jonathan: You're undermining all my advice.

Larry (laughing): Well, I hiked and enjoyed walking. So I suppose I got a decent amount of exercise.

* * *

Crib Notes

1. Your body needs an adequate amount of quality sleep in order to function well. Ensure quantity by sleeping at least seven hours a night. Ensure quality by going to bed by 10:00 pm, which allows for proper melatonin production, leading to better long-term memory storage. Students who go to bed early have significantly higher test scores than students who go to bed late.
2. Exercise also has a big effect on grades. Determine to get daily, rigorous exercise.
3. For great advice on a diet that contributes to wellness and academic performance, peruse the videos on www.nutritionfacts.org, which detail the scientific literature on nutrition.
4. With the guidance of your doctor, consider shifting your diet away from meat, dairy, junk food, and highly processed foods.

Chapter Nine

How to Use Internet, Campus, and Student Resources

Centers, Professors, and Tutors

Many students who find themselves failing college have never used the free resources that their schools offer or that can be found online. They go to college, blunder through their classes, and never seek help. Don't make this mistake. Your college is filled with resources to help you. If these aren't sufficient, the Internet is thick with tips to make your academic life easier.

Your school has probably spent millions of dollars making sure that you have every resource for success at your disposal. Schools sometimes do a poor job of encouraging students to use these resources. Often students don't know about the various programs and centers designed to help them succeed. Worse yet, many students *are* aware that such services exist, but they don't use them. Great students make use of any resources that they need and spend time figuring out what their campuses have to offer.

Counseling Center

The counseling center is happy to talk with you about any issues in your life. Make use of their services. They are bound to confidentiality. No one will know if you go there, and the counselors have the potential to help you through most anything.

Professors

Most professors are in the game of academics because they love students. They want students to succeed and are willing to do almost anything to help them. If you have a question or problem that's not addressed in your syllabus or that a tutor can't help you with, don't hesitate to contact your professor. He or she will most likely be pleased to help. If not, at least you tried. I'll talk more about professors soon, but remember for now that professors are there for you.

Tutors

Your school probably has a small army of tutors who exist to help you. If you need help, go get it. If you're nervous about working with a tutor one-on-one, remember that any pain endured in tutoring will pale in comparison to the annoyance of having to retake classes—not to mention the waste of time and money. Check out your tutoring center and figure out exactly what it offers.

Other Students

Look around your classes. There are students who thoroughly understand the topics studied. They get A's on every test and can answer any in-class question. These are the students you should ask for help. Many of them will be glad to help you figure out tough subjects, because many top students got there by helping others: By teaching information, they reinforced it in their own brains. Consider coaching other students, as it will help you learn, too.

Asking for coaching also helps you befriend top students, who are often well-connected outside of the classroom. They have internships at leading companies, they start clubs and organizations on campus, they launch businesses or are working on important research. Once you get to know them you can offer your help. You never know who's starting the next Facebook or cooking up a cure for neuropathy. Plus, top students are often fascinating people.

Knowing the movers and shakers is also helpful when you want to start something yourself. College can be the perfect time to start a business, because you can find all the skills that you need in the students around you. In addition, professors will often give you free business consultations. They love to see students take initiative and start something great.

Internet Resources

The Internet can help you learn and save you hours of busywork. What follows are a few of my favorite resources, but don't limit yourself to these options. There are hundreds of websites, apps, and tools available to help college students. Do some research and come up with a package of tools that suits your needs. Search Google for "online college tools" and you'll find more of them than any student could ever use.

www.youtube.com

Yes, yes, I know all about YouTube. It's where I can watch skateboarders fall off rails and dogs run in their sleep. If this is the extent of your experience with YouTube, you're missing out on an invaluable resource. Chances are there's a great video explaining almost any problem you have. Go on YouTube, ask, and ye shall receive great instruction. Go therefore and watch no more stupid videos until thy GPA is perfect.

www.khanacademy.org

If you need help with anything math-related, Khan Academy will walk you through it. In addition to videos explaining problems, the site offers software that allows you to practice them. Khan Academy is also branching out into subjects other than math. You'll find resources on economics, finance, organic chemistry, standardized test preparation, and more.

www.tutor.com

Still having trouble? Got some cash to spare? Hop on a website like www.tutor.com. Experts are there to help you twenty-four hours a day in whatever subject you happen to be taking. This site is expensive, though, so try free resources first.

www.google.com

Google may take the prize for being the least-utilized tool because, while every student makes use of it, few students learn how to really wield its power. Do a Google search on "How to use Google" and read a couple of guides. You'll discover that Google can be infinitely more useful to your college life than you imagined. What's more, Google can help you find resources to solve whatever academic problem in which you find yourself. For instance, try searching for ideas to help you memorize anatomy, or master balance sheets, or figure out any other question you might have.

Library

Your campus library, far from being a repository for dusty tomes on the proper soil moisture ratio in almond groves, can be an unparalleled resource in helping you earn great grades.

Librarians these days are highly trained and tech-savvy. They're masters not only at finding information in books, much of which hasn't made it onto the Internet yet, but also at finding resources online. So, the next time you're working on a paper or any other assignment, ask a librarian for help researching your topic. You'll be surprised at how helpful they can be.

Get Professors to Love You

Your professors are a vital resource. They are often on the cutting edge of their disciplines, and they want to teach you exactly what you need to know in order to succeed in life. Professors also love students. Many professors could be making a lot more money in the private sector, but instead of chasing money they are standing in front of you. They want to help you and see you succeed.

They have sacrificed a lot, yet when they teach classes they often see a bunch of bored, listless, whiny, distracted children who would rather be anywhere else. Weekly they deal with cheaters and students begging to have their grades adjusted after they've slacked off in class. Thousands of times professors answer the same questions from students who don't read syllabi. On top of all this they have to deal with the administrative side of their job, get their grading done, come up with activities and assignments for their classes, etc.

Being a professor is hard.

So you come along and want the professor to like you. You recognize that your professor is well connected in the community, and you know how valuable it would be if she thought you were the most awesome student to darken her doorway in years. What do you do to impress your professor?

You're partway there just by thinking about what the professor puts up with. You don't want to annoy her. Next, you want to figure out what she wants, and then provide it.

So what do professors really want? They want to see students who:

- Get excited about the subject taught
- Appreciate how much work they do
- Recognize and respect them as people
- Are respectful and attentive in class
- Do well on assignments and tests
- Are honest

I know someone whose dissertation focused on this topic, and he found that professors value conscientiousness over any other attribute. So don't give them any reason to suspect that you are dishonest or that you cut corners. If you live up to all the abovementioned expectations, your professors will likely respond well to you.

Sit at the front of the class to show your eagerness to learn. You'll have the added benefit of avoiding the distractions of everything going on in the room. Always be attentive, and actively participate in class discussions. Conjure up questions to ask professors after class. Ask where you can learn more about some topic that interests you. Find material online that's relevant to your classes and forward it to your professors. Thank the professors for all the work they have done to help you learn.

By doing these things, you'll demonstrate that you're fascinated by the topics taught and want to learn more. Professors love students who get interested in the material. As an added benefit, by acting as though you're fascinated by a topic, you will likely become more interested in it. Don't work too hard to fake interest—professors have great acting detectors—but by asking questions and attempting to engage with the material, you will come across as more interested than the student who shows no signs of life.

What if you're shy? There's no need to lead class discussions or be that one student who raises his hand in answer to every in-class question. You can show that you're engaged simply by asking the professor a couple of thoughtful questions after class.

Do this with all of your professors. Soon, if you need a job, a recommendation, or some information, you have a network of geniuses who will move heaven and earth to help you. Remember that only 1% of people in the western world have a PhD. Your campus is crawling with them. Imagine having a whole network of the most educated people in the world at your disposal. This network's potential value is in the millions. Work diligently toward gaining your professors' attention and respect.

Professors will also love your proper classroom etiquette.

Many college students have awful classroom etiquette. They surf Facebook, do other homework, text, talk to each other, and often ignore professors. Some professors know how to demand the class's attention, but others don't. What students fail to realize is that they are only hurting themselves with bad behavior.

Unfortunately, some classes are criminally boring. Professors may not know how to engage a classroom: their voices are monotone, and lecture is a painful experience for everyone. But it's still not cool to waste class time on Facebook. First, it's rude to the professor and to the other students who are trying to pay attention. Second, the professor will think less of you. Even a boring professor might be able and willing to get you a job in two seconds if they think you're a fantastic person who would benefit a friend's business. So no matter what, don't diminish a professor's perception of you by acting disrespectfully in class.

Even if you do make the conscious decision to dismiss what your professor or other students think of you, at least spend that time reading the textbook. You owe it to yourself to get educated even if your professor isn't up to par.

Another thing you can do if your classes are boring is use your own creativity to spice up the classroom. Look up great videos that are relevant to the class and ask your professor if you can play them for everyone. The professor might be delighted. Www.ted.com is a great resource for such videos. Or find someone who would be a great guest speaker and ask your professor to bring them in.

Top Students in Their Own Words: Robert, PhD, Research and Statistical Methodology: University of Alabama

Jonathan: What made you a great student?

Robert: I had a rule: I never, never, never, left a classroom until I understood *everything* that was presented. If I didn't understand each concept and, more importantly, why that concept was important, I would stay after class and question the professor until I felt confident that I thoroughly understood every point that had been discussed.

Jonathan: How would you remember those concepts? Did you take notes or anything?

Robert: Taking notes was a big part of it. I took copious notes during class and also wrote down any questions that came to my mind. If those questions weren't answered during the lecture, I would approach the professor afterward and ask all my questions. I also took extensive notes from my post-class talks with my professors.

Each evening before going to bed, I would rewrite and organize all my notes. Once again, I would make sure that I had a thorough understanding of each concept. If I discovered any gaps in my understanding while rewriting my notes, I would go to class early and ask the professor about it.

Jonathan: How did you study for tests?

Robert: Preparing for exams was easy. I would simply look over my notes once or twice to refresh what I already knew and thoroughly understood. I didn't need to study more because I had learned the information so well the day of class. All I needed was a little refresher. I hardly ever opened a textbook as long as my notes were thorough.

Jonathan: Do you think that asking professors a lot of questions made them like you?

Robert: No question about it. Perhaps the best thing about this approach was the relationships I developed with my professors. There was never a professor who was bothered by my incessant questioning. In fact, it rather endeared me to them. They loved my enthusiasm and curiosity, and they were always willing to help. Even now that I'm out of school I maintain close relationships with many of my former professors.

* * *

Crib Notes

1. Put together a package of programs, apps, and websites that will help you in college. Use the resources mentioned in this chapter and look around for others.
2. Explore the tutoring and counseling options that your school offers, and then make use of them. Also, get to know professors and top students. Most will be happy to help you with almost any problem.
3. Get your professors to love you by sitting at the front of the class, showing respect to the professor and your classmates, and practicing proper classroom etiquette. Show unreasonable enthusiasm for the subject by asking the professor questions after class and forwarding relevant articles.

Chapter Ten

How To Increase Personal Productivity Without Burning Out

Prioritize

Most students fail to prioritize. They wander through their days doing whatever seems important in the moment. But what seems important in the moment may not be the thing that will propel you closer to what you really want. A great way to battle this problem is to prioritize.

You know what you should be doing. If you want to be a painter, your number one job is to put brush to canvas. If you want to be a pro snowboarder, you get out on the slopes. If you want to be a great student, your top priorities are getting in enough spaced exposures to dominate your exams and scheduling enough short writing sessions to let your subconscious do the work for you in the between-times on papers and presentations.

So why do students waste hours on Facebook, watch brain cell-massacring shows on MTV, and count the tack holes on their dorm room walls? Because they don't prioritize.

You must prioritize daily in order to be highly effective. Each morning, before busying yourself with anything else, write down everything that you need to do during the day. As soon as you're done, compare this list with your academic and life goals. You'll immediately notice that some of the activities on your list are far more connected to achieving your dreams than others.

Now start a new list. Pick the one thing that you can do today that will help you most in your academics, and make it number one. Next, pick the most important thing you can do for your life goals and write that down as number two. Continue in this manner until your priority list is organized in descending order of importance. Once your list is done, work on number one until it's complete. Remember, this is the most important thing you can do today, so don't let anything else get in the way. Once you've knocked number one out, start working on number two. Continue in this fashion for the rest of the day. Even if you don't get everything done, you'll have accomplished the absolutely most important actions.

When you prioritize, every day of your life will become far more productive and enjoyable than before (make sure to prioritize an activity or two that will give you enjoyment, too). Now that you're getting important stuff done in less time than before, you have more time to spend on sports, social events, and other activities that are vital to your well-being. Better yet, if you start the day accomplishing the most important tasks, you are free to enjoy less obviously productive activities, such as socializing, for the rest of the day. You can relax because you're not worried about important tasks that you failed to accomplish. Small stuff is easy to forget about, but the important stuff weighs heavily on your mind, robbing you of true relaxation and enjoyment.

Prioritizing also helps eliminate non-starter syndrome. This condition affects countless people whose intellect and imagination help them conceive fantastic ideas. Yet those same smarts turn around and betray their hosts by thinking up a million reasons that the ideas won't work. The mind becomes paralyzed by the size of the task and doesn't know where to start. People stuck in this situation find it difficult to take concrete steps toward their goals.

Prioritization forces you to break down large, nebulous ideas into chunks that you can accomplish daily. And as long as you place those chunks at the top of your priority list and do nothing else until they are finished, you will complete the whole task. The best way to eat an elephant is one bite at a time.

A word of caution: Now that you have a prioritized daily list, don't get too crazy about sticking to it. You will always have interruptions and last-minute opportunities for fun. A lot of the benefit from this exercise comes simply from identifying what you really want and what you need to do in order to get it. Even if you don't knock out your entire to-do list every day, try to at least do the two most important things, and you'll steadily move toward your ideal future. But don't let The List ruin your joy in the moment. A little personal messiness is okay, and life is more fun if you're not endlessly tied to to-dos.

Distractions

"We have met the enemy and he is us."
—*Walt Kelly*

The two worst time-sucking black holes are found on desks and small stands in most dorm rooms. They are the TV and the Internet. You know this, but allow me to climb atop my soapbox for a moment and remind you of a few things. Soon, you're going to leave the comfortable, forgiving world of academia and be thrown unceremoniously into real life. There, you'll be expected to act, think, and work like an adult.

You have exactly one job in college: to prepare yourself for the rest of your life. The rest of your life will largely be determined by how well you do in college. You'll soon have to support yourself, and maybe other people. How well you support them might be proportional to the effort you expended in college and soon afterward.

Exactly how many times do you need to watch *Harry Potter*, or *The Hangover*, or reruns of *How I Met Your Mother*? How many of these movies and shows does it take to make a life complete?

The computer is equally offensive. How many hours have you spent playing *World of Warcraft*, *Counter-Strike*, or *Call of Duty*? How many checking Facebook?

Occasionally it's great to blow off steam by enjoying a movie, game, or show. But many students trade college education and a better future for passive entertainment. You don't want to make a similar mistake.

Crib Notes

1. Each morning, write down everything you need to do that day. After comparing these tasks with your academic and personal goals, create a priority list, starting with the most important task. By following this list, you will always get the most important stuff done.
2. Limit your time with passive entertainment—such as video games and movies—that aren't helping you achieve your goals.

Chapter Eleven

How to Enjoy College

Work Smarter, not Harder

I'm all about freeing up time so that you can enjoy college. We are meant to enjoy life. If at any point in life you find yourself consistently without joy, consider some changes. A good salary, for instance, isn't worth a job that makes you miserable. In the same way, if you find yourself hating college, it's time to evaluate whether or not you're wasting precious life. Change your major. Do something different.

The solution to misery at college or a job isn't laziness; sometimes working hard and temporarily denying yourself pleasure is necessary. But consider having some mandatory enjoyment in college. By working smarter, not harder, you'll accomplish more than most people and still have time to do other things.

Choosing the Right School

This is a fairly useless section, is it not? After all, Harvard, Stanford, and Yale are the best schools for you, right?

Yeah, the Ivy Leagues are awesome. If you have even the slightest chance of going, by all means, go for it. If you don't have the highest GPA but you've lived a well-rounded life, apply. The Ivy Leagues like to populate their halls with valedictorians as well as with those who have diverse backgrounds and experiences.

But be warned. If you're not a valedictorian, you might get into a Yale or a Princeton and struggle. At the undergraduate level you'll most likely have limited access to the faculty and deans, and you'll be competing with people who were not only born with silver spoons in their mouths but with college success guides tucked under their arms as well.

If you're normal like most other people, consider going to a small liberal arts school during your undergraduate years. Discover one that specializes in what you want to major in and you'll find yourself surrounded by people like you, which will help you feel right at home. With careful effort and a lot of study, you will be one of the top students at the school. This will give you unparalleled access to faculty and deans. For instance, at my liberal arts school, I had the cell phone numbers of all my professors and could walk into the dean's office whenever he was around. That small, personal, family-like environment doesn't exist in all the big institutions. What's more, you won't be competing against an army of valedictorians.

If you go the small liberal arts route, you can be a big fish in a small pond. Then, when it comes time for graduate school, you will have the recommendations, grades, and background needed to get into a prestigious university. For example, I barely squeaked into my university. But after learning these college success principles, I was able to excel, even to the point of winning the President's Award. Now I'm a strong candidate to pursue a graduate degree at a more prestigious school.

If private schools aren't an option, spend serious time looking at your state colleges and universities. Like private schools, they vary drastically in focus, values, and quality. Taking the time to find the school that best fits your goals and personality may take a while. Don't fall for the idea that you must choose between the Ivy Leagues and whatever university lies within fifty miles of your house. There are thousands of universities around. A handful of them will be a perfect fit for you and can lead to great joy in your college years. It's worth the time to choose carefully.

Two Ways to Enjoy College and Life

We either make ourselves miserable, or we make ourselves strong. The amount of work is the same.

— *Carlos Castaneda*

Enjoyment comes in at least two varieties: decadent and beneficial. Decadent activities are those we enjoy simply for enjoyment's sake. What's decadent for each person varies depending on their goals in life, but I include watching movies and sports and playing video games in this category, as well as staring at the wall, and hanging out with people who don't actively encourage me to be a better person. It's fun to chill out, deteriorate on the couch, and watch something. Decadent activities are important, but enjoy them in small doses. Too much decadence can slow you down and drain the confidence that you can do anything useful.

Beneficial activities bring enjoyment but also add something immediately apparent to your life or to the lives of others. For me, mountain biking is a beneficial activity. It brings me joy and excitement, but it also provides exercise, benefitting my mind and body. Watching TV feels like nothing more than an escape; reading a novel provides the same (if not better) escape, but it also engages my imagination and teaches me language skills. Win, win, win. I also enjoy creating art, which not only gives me the thrill and fulfillment of exercising my creativity but also makes me feel as though I'm contributing to the world. With art, there's even the possibility of selling my work. If you work toward mastering one of your hobbies, one day it might turn into your primary source of income. What could be better than that?

To maximize your success and enjoyment in college, choose recreational activities from both categories but focus on those that bring not only joy but also other benefits.

Travel

Since starting college I have traveled to sixteen different states in the US and have visited eleven countries. Experiences I've had in each place have stayed with me more strongly than any I've had on my college campus.

How could I ever forget slipping on algae and falling into a Venetian canal at 11:30 pm in the middle of winter and then laughing until it hurt? Or waking up in a sixteenth-century castle overlooking Florence? Listening to a Christmas concert in Oslo? Eating sauerkraut under a propane heater at an outdoor market in Munich? Watching the sunset from the fortified wall of a Roman-era castle on a hill in Sagunto, Spain? Climbing a windswept hill to look over a majestic valley in Scotland's Isle of Skye? Almost being pick-pocketed by a gypsy woman on a French metro? Eating fresh, stone oven-baked bread from a basement bakery on a tiny side street in Morocco? Standing in the majesty of St. Peter's Basilica, or staring at the beautiful ceiling in the Sistine Chapel?

All of these memories spring from one trip. My wife, my brother, a close friend, and I journeyed to Sagunto, Spain for one quarter of school to study Spanish. On weekends and breaks we traveled all over Europe. We took in the most breathtaking cathedrals, landscapes, and historical stories. We ate incredible food, met loving people, and gained a new perspective on this world that we all call home.

If you have a chance to study abroad, take it. In fact, ensure that you have the chance. Study-abroad tuition is usually cheaper than standard tuition and, with a little bit of planning, it's possible to travel cheaply once you arrive in a new place. You will never regret seeing the world, and there's no better time to do it than while you're in college, before a job and a family can make it difficult to leave home. Such an experience will broaden your mind and whet your appetite for adventure.

Don't even think about using the excuse that studying abroad will set you back credit-wise. Who cares if you get set back one quarter or one year? When you're sixty-five, will it matter if you've worked for forty-two years or forty-three? Better yet, if you go for only one quarter or semester, you might not get set back at all, as classes taken abroad can count as electives.

Jocks, Nerds, Partiers, Saints, and Perfect People

Watch any college movie and you'll see a diverse cast of characters: jocks, nerds, partiers, saints, jerks, and a couple of "perfect" people. It's this great mix of personalities and lifestyles that makes college such an interesting place.

In college, you get to choose what kind of person you'll be. You'll likely have left your insular high school world where all your friends, family members, and community people know you and have you labeled. Such labeling is hard to fight.

You're in college now, surrounded by hundreds of people who have no preconceived ideas about who you are. You also have more freedom to make your own decisions. And what are we but the sum of our decisions? Realizing this frees you to become, well, you—the real you that you want to be.

So who do you want to be?

A huge part of who we are and who we will become arises from our environments. It has been said that people are a composite of their five closest friends, mirroring them in temperament, weight, finances, outlook, and mood. Some people say that this is because like attracts like, and I believe that's true to a certain extent, but I also believe people can change drastically under the influence of their environments.

Those you choose to surround yourself with will largely dictate who you are, which is good news, because you now have the power to choose who you will become. If you want drama, you can have it. If you want a self-destructive, carefree lifestyle, hang out with those kinds of people. If you want adventure, success, and love, you can have that, too.

From this point on, almost everything that happens in your life will be your fault, arising from the people and the environment you surround yourself with as well as the tenor of your own thoughts. So choose encouraging, loving, giving, service-oriented people to surround yourself with and your life will follow in their footprints.

A Day of Rest

I believe the Sabbath; I keep the Sabbath.
— *John Harvey Kellogg*

Like a path through the forest, Sabbath creates a marker for ourselves so, if we are lost, we can find our way back to our center.
— *Wayne Muller*

The meaning of the Sabbath is to celebrate time rather than space. Six days a week we live under the tyranny of things of space; on the Sabbath we try to become attuned to holiness in time. It is a day on which we are called upon to share in what is eternal in time, to turn from the results of creation to the mystery of creation; from the world of creation to the creation of the world.
— *Abraham Joshua Heschel*

The Sabbath is perhaps the oldest Judeo-Christian tradition. Genesis records that God, right after completing creation, rested on the seventh day and blessed it as a perpetual reminder of His efforts. God later recorded the Sabbath in the Ten Commandments, which were given to Moses. While on earth, Christ kept the Sabbath and, after Christ's death, his disciples faithfully followed the tradition.

The Sabbath is one of the most controversial commandments in the Biblical canon. After setting it aside as a blessed day—a day of rest, celebration, and communion with God—some people became so obsessive about keeping the Sabbath that doing almost anything but standing still was considered breaking it. Jesus tried to correct this misunderstanding, which is one of the reasons He was crucified. A few hundred years later, the dominant Christian church at the time decided to change the Sabbath from Saturday to Sunday. Most Christians eventually adopted this change, and it wasn't long before some were persecuting others for not worshiping on Sunday. Controversy over the Sabbath and its proper observance is ongoing with no end in sight.

It's funny how God says, "Take a weekly day of rest and be nice to each other," and people proceed to make the day of rest a misery and persecute those who observe it differently.

So what's the deal with this controversial day, and why does it show up in a book about college?

I believe the Sabbath is a priceless gift to humanity, and to college students in particular. It made my college life a lot more enjoyable, and I know many other students who feel the same. Not one to hold back valuable advice, I now ask you to consider observing a Sabbath—even a Sabbath detached from religion. I believe you'll find it one of the best things you can do for your personal sanity and well-being.

Before saying any more, I will step aside and allow God, who holds the patent for the idea of the Sabbath, to define it. This, the fourth commandment, is found in Exodus 20:8-11:

> Remember the Sabbath day, to keep it holy. Six days you shall labor, and do all your work, but the seventh day is a Sabbath to the Lord your God. On it you shall not do any work, you, or your son, or your daughter, your male servant, or your female servant, or your livestock, or the sojourner who is within your gates· For in six days the Lord made heaven and earth, the sea, and all that is in them, and rested on the seventh day. Therefore the Lord blessed the Sabbath day and made it holy.

As I mentioned above, people interpret this commandment in a number of ways, some of which aren't healthy. So how can we do it right?

First, realize that most believers see God in one of two ways: either as an angry dictator, or as a loving father. People interpret God's commandments according to where they see God on the angry dictator-loving father continuum. If you view God as a tyrannical, angry being, you're likely to observe His commandments carefully but with a weighty sense of dread. If you see God as a loving father, you look upon His commandments as priceless advice. Instead of following them out of fear, you recognize that God wants the best for you, and by observing His advice your life will improve.

My standpoint on the issue is probably already clear: since studying the Bible seriously, I've come to see God as a loving father. As I study the canon of scripture, I can't shake the feeling that God is watching out for our well-being. Each of His directives is meant to make life happier. Imagine what would happen if we actually followed the advice He put forward in the Golden Rule (do unto others what you would want them to do unto you), which Christ called the greatest of all laws. Many of the world's problems would vanish overnight.

So let's look at the Sabbath from the priceless advice perspective. Here's my "translation" (using supporting material from other parts of the Bible): "Every week from Friday at sunset to Saturday at sunset, take a vacation from the norm. Forget your homework. You have six days to work on that. Also, forget your other common tasks like going to work, mowing the lawn, and cleaning the house. Finally, don't waste the day doing normal things like watching TV or staring at your phone. Today is special. A day of rest from your normal life. Get outside. Go to the mountains and take a walk. Connect with nature, which I have provided for your enjoyment. Visit your family. Volunteer with an organization that helps the poor, homeless, and hungry (for as you do unto the least of these, you do it unto me). Go to church and spend some time with me, for I have missed you during your busy week."

That's the Sabbath that many others and I enjoy. It's a time to disconnect from everything that's stressful, a day of fellowship with community and friends. It's a day of mountain biking and hiking. It's a day of reading the Bible and learning more about how to lead a peaceful, fulfilling life. Best of all, it's a much-needed day of rest.

Some people choose to use the Sabbath as a digital fast. They turn off their phones and tablets, avoid the computer, and never turn on the TV, giving them more time to engage in the parts of life that don't rely on binary code.

Each week I look forward to the Sabbath and cherish each moment of the freedom inherent in it. Sometimes, when I have been traveling or have had a busy concert schedule, it feels as though I have skipped Sabbath. It's an awful feeling, as if I failed to keep an appointment with my best friend.

If you haven't discovered the joy of the Sabbath, I encourage you to observe it for a couple of months. Take a weekly vacation from regular life. You deserve and need it. You'll find that, after an escape, you will return to life rested, refreshed, and ready to succeed. Matthew 11:28-29 says: "Come to me, all you who are weary and burdened, and I will give you rest. Take my yoke upon you and learn from me, for I am gentle and humble in heart, and you will find rest for your souls."

On the Sabbath, enjoy rest for your soul.

Crib Notes

1. Keep an open mind about what school to go to. Don't fall into the false choice of "it's the Ivy League or the college down the street." Take the time to find a school that perfectly fits who you are and who you want to be.
2. To get the most out of college and life, focus on beneficial activities. Enjoy decadent activities sparingly. Determine which enjoyable activities are most fulfilling to you by asking yourself which ones add to the world, improve the lives of others, and have the potential to bring you financial freedom.
3. You are a composite of the people you spend time with. Choose what kind of life you want to have by hanging out with people who already live that life.
4. Travel. There's a whole world of adventure out there. A great way to experience the world is to study abroad. Check with your school. If it doesn't have a study-abroad program, find a program that you can join.
5. Take a weekly Sabbath—a day in which you avoid all homework, work, and anything that commonly takes up your time. Go into nature; spend time with people you normally don't get to see. Do volunteer work. Go to church. Spend time with God. Then return to regular life rested and refreshed.

Chapter Twelve

Finding Work During or After College

Is College Worth It?

You've no doubt heard people yakking about how many college grads are unemployed or underemployed. These people also question whether college is worth it. After all, why not just learn a skill and spend those four years making money and gaining experience instead of throwing money at the sticky fingers in the ivory tower?

Recently, the Gallup organization published a piece called "Is College Worth It?" Based on their research, they found that college graduates not only make a lot more money over the course of their careers than non-grads do, but they also find more meaningful careers, which leads to an increase in social, physical, and communal well-being. If you want happiness and a rewarding, financially successful life, college is for you.

So now you're graduating and you want to find that meaningful career that leads you through fields of puppies under rainbow skies with the occasional unicorn prancing by. What can you do in college to ensure that afterward, you'll find such a career?

A Body of Work

Good hiring managers have discovered the best indicator of who will make a great employee: accomplishments. No matter how eloquently you state that you're a "people person," or that you're "highly motivated," your accomplishments speak louder than your words. After all, if you're such a highly motivated people person, shouldn't you have a resounding record of what those qualities have helped you achieve?

College is a great time to build a record of accomplishment. There are many ways to do this:

- Start a club
- Help a professor conduct research
- Write articles for school or regional newspapers
- Organize an event
- Get a great guest speaker to come speak to your department
- Win contests
- Start a business
- Invent something
- Volunteer at a non-profit
- Get an internship
- Get a job

These are examples from things students around me did. A couple of students I know actually did everything on this list. But the list can be as long as your imagination allows. Simply start getting involved and keep track of what you get done.

Accomplishing things on campus will bring great advantages. Professors start talking about you in faculty meetings. Other students become aware of your existence. The local paper may cover your event, which is always proof that you're a mover and a shaker. Best of all, by getting involved and getting things done, you will get in the habit of accomplishing things. Make no mistake, accomplishment, like laziness, is a habit. You'll be much happier if you get into the accomplishment habit.

Need ideas for something to do or ways to get involved? Look at the records of entrepreneurs. Great entrepreneurs see the world differently than the rest of us. When computers came out, most people said, "Wow! Look at this amazing technology!" Steve Jobs looked at the computer and said, "This is good, but it could be *way* better."

To entrepreneurs, everything is broken.

When something is broken—be it technology, your school paper, or anything else around you—start looking for ways to fix or improve it. By remembering that *everything* is broken, you'll begin to see hundreds of ways to get involved, and hundreds of things you can do, invent, or change to make the world a better place.

Proving Your Worth

Put yourself in the shoes of the people who might give you a job. Hiring you is terrifying. Sure, your résumé might look good and you might present yourself well, but they really have no way of knowing what you'll be like as an employee. If they hire you and things don't work out, it can cost them tens of thousands to hundreds of thousands of dollars in lost productivity. On the other hand, if you're a rock star of an employee, you can make the company hundreds of thousands to millions of dollars.

Thus, those tasked with hiring people grasp at anything they can in order to get a sense for who is sitting across the desk. How can you prove that you'll be a rock star employee?

As we just discussed, actions speak louder than words. Perhaps one of the best ways to show you'd be a great employee is to take action to show how badly you want it.

I'll use my brother as an example. As I type this sentence, one week has passed since he got hired as a full-time firefighter for the city of Oxnard, California. Over 2,000 people applied for the job. Only nine were hired.

My brother knew that thousands would be competing for the position, so he worked hard to prove his worth. First of all, he was well qualified. He has worked as an emergency medical technician for the past three years and part-time as a paid-call firefighter for one year. He recently graduated with his bachelor's degree in management. But he knew that hundreds of other applicants would have similar or even better qualifications, so he knew he'd have to do more to stand out.

Before applying for the position, he drove three hours to Oxnard on two separate days and visited all eight of the city's fire stations. He talked to all the firefighters and captains at each station. He memorized how many and what kinds of trucks each station used. He studied the geographic areas served by each station and found out how many people lived in those districts, as well as their demographical composition. He read about the history of Oxnard and its fire department. He studied what percentages of the department's resources were devoted to brush fires, structure fires, water rescues, and medical responses.

When my brother was interviewed for the position, he knew almost everything there was to know about the department. He proved by his actions that he wanted the position a great deal and was willing to do the careful, detailed work required of a firefighter.

Demonstrate that level of eagerness and thoroughness to your potential employers. You will impress them.

Learn Skills

While hiring managers love to see a record of accomplishment and eagerness, they also love to see candidates with skills that will add value to their company.

Your major's required classes will teach you amazing skills, but you'll soon discover that you're competing for jobs against a thousand other people with your exact major, and perhaps many people with master's degrees.

The way you differentiate yourself is through your skills. Let's say that you're a criminal justice major and you want to be a police officer. You take all of the required classes, but in addition to that you spend a year abroad studying Spanish and take an elective to become certified in conflict resolution. Not only did you have a blast studying abroad and then learning awesome life skills from your conflict resolution class, but now you're bilingual and certified in a skill that's invaluable to police officers. You suddenly look a lot better than the guy who put "good communicator" and "self-starter" under the skills section of his résumé.

Study your chosen career. Talk to people working in it. Identify what skills make someone a valuable employee and see how many of those skills you can acquire by taking electives.

Playing the Game

In addition to having a record of accomplishment, a stack of skills, and a way to prove your worth and eagerness, you'll also improve your odds of finding the perfect career by learning the rules and best practices in the game of job hunting.

During my senior year in college, I worked with one of my school's business law faculty members to start a career resource center in the School of Business. My first responsibility was to create a library of career resources. I read more than a dozen of the top-rated books on job hunting, résumé crafting, and career advice so that I could help students locate the information they were looking for. I also spent hours editing résumés and conducting mock interviews with job-seeking students.

What became clear is that there's a complex art and science behind job hunting, as well as a set of best practices that can be the difference between getting hired quickly in a great career or struggling for a long time to find work.

In his wonderful book *What Color Is Your Parachute?*, Richard N. Bolles explains that a vast majority of advertised job openings have already been filled. The company is simply going through the legal requirements of posting the job and conducting interviews, but they already know who they plan to hire. Thus, blindly sending your résumé all over the place is the worst way to find a job, because almost every job you apply for has already been given to someone else. Knowing this fact can save you hundreds of hours of job searching.

Looking for a job? Or an internship? It's time to start learning the best practices for the job hunt, and there are dozens of them. Go to your campus career center. Their staff should be able to help you craft a great résumé, practice your interview skills, coach you on how to dress, and give you countless other helpful suggestions.

You must also read *What Color is Your Parachute?* by Richard N. Bolles. If everyone would take the time to read that book and put its principles into practice, unemployment wouldn't be such a big issue in this country. Another timeless book that can help you think outside the box in your job search and in life is Napoleon Hill's *Think and Grow Rich.* I guarantee both books are worth your time.

Crib Notes

1. Actions speak louder than words. Spend your college years accomplishing things so you'll have a body of work to prove that you're a "highly motivated people person."
2. Prove your worth by going the extra mile to impress your potential employers. Shock them with your knowledge of the company and your determination to prove that you're the best person for the job.
3. Skills are ways in which you contribute to a company. Focus your electives on classes that teach you concrete skills. For example, learn Photoshop, conflict resolution, a second language, lab skills, and so on.
4. Read great resources on careers and job-hunting, such as *What Color Is Your Parachute?* by Richard N. Bolles and *Think and Grow Rich* by Napoleon Hill.

Afterword

After choosing death instead of exile or a vow of silence, Socrates is reported to have said, "The unexamined life is not worth living."

I think life's pretty great whether or not you sit around examining its every facet. But Socrates has a point: Examining our lives leads to living more worthwhile lives.

We've spent a lot of time looking at the minutiae of how to live well in the peculiar, complex world of college. My sincerest hope is that this examination will help you become a whole person who participates fully in all realms of life. As an educated person, you will have a tremendous amount of power, more than the majority of all individuals throughout history. You'll have an understanding of the world that will allow you to add value to the economy, your community, your family, and to the richness of your own intellectual life. That's a very compelling future, one worth the hard work of excelling in college.

So learn everything and examine everything. Plant your feet on the solid foundations of gentleness and kindness. Be helpful, positive, and encouraging to all you come into contact with. Do all this and college will be numbered among the best and most exhilarating years of your life.

Acknowledgments

Several people have my deepest gratitude for making this book a reality. First and foremost, Lisa Fast deserves more appreciation than words can convey. You taught me a study technique that changed my college experience from a failing and frustrating one into a triumphant one. Without you, I might not have finished college, much less excelled in it. Thank you for saving my academic career and for giving me the opportunity to live an extraordinary life.

Thank you, Pamela Dietrich, for reading an early draft of this book and for having the courage to tell me that it was terrible. Your insights and editorial skills pushed me to do better work. Sometimes honesty is painful, both to give and to receive, yet you managed honesty alongside encouragement, which made all the difference.

To my wife and family: thank you for loving and supporting me, both when I was failing and when I was succeeding. It's said that you can't choose your family, but if given the opportunity, I'd pick you all again.

Laura Melchor, thank you for being a perfect editor. You navigated the jungles of the English language with great skill and yet somehow managed to step far enough away from the minutiae to vastly improve the larger ideas and themes. It's always a pleasure to interact with a lover of words, especially one as passionate, kind, and professional as you.

Finally, I wish to thank everyone who allowed me to interview them for this book or who in other ways contributed to its creation. You are many, yet somehow each of you is the best.

Crib Notes

Chapter One

The Spacing Effect

1. Space study time to allow the brain to create and develop effective connections. Allow several hours to several days between repetitions, though one day is usually optimal.
2. To get the maximum number of exposures, read assigned chapters before class, attend lectures, and read your lecture notes before going to bed. These three steps will start the spacing effect process.
3. Prepare for exams by reviewing all test materials, such as textbook chapters and lecture notes, once a day for a minimum of five days. Don't "study"—simply read through everything once. Five to seven exposures got me an A on difficult tests. Experiment to find your ideal number.

Chapter Two

Surveying

1. Read a textbook chapter in its entirety.
2. Do spaced chapter reviews, or surveys, by reading only titles, boxes, graphs, and photo captions; bulleted, italicized, or underlined text; and the topic sentence in each paragraph (usually the first sentence: if not, mark the topic sentence on your initial

reading so you can find it later). Finish by reading the chapter summary. Finally, read your lecture notes.

3. Enjoy the hours this technique can save you.

Chapter Three

Math

1. Write down all steps for a math problem in English. Be specific, covering every step.
2. Write down an example problem and each possible variation. Include enough examples to make sure you can translate the English instructions into actual math.
3. When prepping for a test, review those written instructions and the selected examples daily until you have them memorized. Remember, it's not the amount of time spent studying that counts: it's the number of spaced exposures. Don't "study": just read over everything once per day.
4. Still need help? Turn to the Internet. Use YouTube, www.khanacademy.org, and everything else on there that can help you. Just remember that you can't use the Internet on the test.

Faster Reading

1. To increase reading speed, eliminate vocalization. Make sure that your lips, tongue, and throat aren't trying to pronounce words as you read. Any vocalization limits your reading speed to the speed at which you can speak.
2. Push the voice in your head to read at a faster rate. By constantly pushing this voice, your comfortable reading speed will eventually increase to about eight hundred words per minute or more. Reading faster also increases comprehension, as you will link ideas together before you can forget them.

Note Taking

1. Read all assigned chapters and readings before the lecture. Now you can take notes only on what outside materials don't cover, freeing up your time to really listen to the lecture.
2. Don't write down notes while reading your textbook. If you write anything, write down questions for your professor.
3. Review notes when surveying related chapters.

Writing

1. To master writing, read more. Exposing your brain to all a language can do will improve your spelling, grammar, and vocabulary.
2. Carefully study your English textbook and pay attention in class to learn the rules of proper English .
3. Take advantage of your campus's writing center to get feedback on your writing.
4. If you need to take drastic measures, copy magazine articles by hand into a notebook.
5. Vary your sentence length to keep your writing interesting.
6. Use small words and small sentences, and write in the active voice.
7. Make sure your writing sounds similar to speech, but more polished.
8. Don't just puke ink onto pages. Value your work and put your best efforts into creating something you're proud to turn in.

Chapter Four

Boosting Creativity

1. For big papers and projects, give your subconscious permission to do the work for you. Instead of forcing your brain to come up with all the pages in one sitting, work on your paper for only a few minutes per day far ahead of the due date. Your subconscious will

use the extra time to search for answers, new directions, and new associations to bring into the paper.

2. Spend a few minutes working on a project as soon as it's assigned. Read the prompt several times, write down any ideas that come to you, and try to write a partial outline or introduction. Now that your subconscious knows what needs to be in the paper, it will search for ideas and sources in other classes and readings.

Building a Knowledge Base

1. The more you know, the more you can learn. The mind hangs new information on the knowledge frameworks it already possesses, so the more knowledge you have, the easier it is for your brain to make associations with new information. Thus, read deeply and widely to gain as much knowledge as possible.

Reading for Sources

1. Read a variety of high-quality books and publications. You'll develop well-rounded opinions that look great in papers, have tons of sources already identified for many topics, and develop a knowledge base that will help you learn new things at a fast rate. Also, papers are difficult to write only if you have nothing to say. Wide reading will give you plenty to say.

Chapter Five

Mastering Science with Associations, Mnemonics, and The Spacing Effect

1. Learning science will greatly increase your intellectual enjoyment in life, not to mention give you the skills to exist in our technologically advanced society. Learn to love science.

2. Science requires memorizing details, so lean heavily on the spacing effect. Read assigned chapters before class, marking anything that seems important. Go to class and take good notes, and then review those notes before going to bed. Later, create a cheat sheet in your notebook and record everything you suspect you'll need to know for tests, such as facts, formulas, questions from the homework, and more. Review this cheat sheet daily until the spacing effect helps you memorize all the important details.
3. Learn to use associations and mnemonics to help you remember complex lists and number sets.

Chapter Six

Taking Tests

1. Preparation is 95% of the battle. If you are thoroughly prepared, the test will not be an issue. Use the spacing effect and surveys to get at least eight to ten spaced exposures to everything that could be on a test.
2. Once in a test, read all questions before answering anything. Let your subconscious get to work. This is especially important for essay questions. Trust your preparation and skip this step if time is limited.
3. Answer the easiest questions first. This puts you in a relaxed mood, giving your mind permission to work at peak performance.
4. Don't get hung up on one question. If the answer doesn't come quickly, it probably won't come at all. Put a mark beside the question. If you have extra time later, come back to it.
5. Don't second-guess multiple choice or true or false questions. Your first impression is usually the right one.
6. Do recheck data entry questions, formulas, and essay answers. Often a tiny mistake in data entry or formulas will throw off the whole problem. Essays can always be expanded or tightened.

Chapter Seven

Small Study Hacks

1. To improve the quality of your study time, eliminate all distractions. Multitasking reduces your efficiency. Think of multitasking as multidistracting. Find a quiet place and focus.
2. Stay away from most study groups. Conducting conversations unrelated to the subject at hand makes you lose twice: you don't enjoy your conversation because you know you should be studying, and you don't get any studying done because you're talking too much.
3. Technical classes are the exception to the above rule. Classmates can help you solve complex formulas and data-heavy problems. Such help can save you hours in the homework phase, giving you more time to review.
4. Don't take any bad classes. Ask around, research online, and sign up for more classes than you will take (just make sure adding extra classes doesn't impact your financial aid). Drop any class that threatens to be a misery. If you have to take a hard class, seek out a professor who is irrationally in love with the topic and is great at spreading that love.
5. Take a ten-minute study break every fifty minutes and do something active. This is an easy way to trick your brain into thinking, "I don't have to study for three hours, just for fifty minutes."
6. Love what you do. Make an effort to become fascinated with every class you take. If your program is consistently dragging you down, however, carefully consider changing your major. Perhaps there's a major out there that will engage your mind so you'll love going to classes every day.
7. Don't skip class. Go to every class. Just do it. Your grades will thank you.

Chapter Eight

Lifestyle

1. Your body needs an adequate amount of quality sleep in order to function well. Ensure quantity by sleeping at least seven hours a night. Ensure quality by going to bed by 10:00 pm, which allows for proper melatonin production, leading to better long-term memory storage. Students who go to bed early have significantly higher test scores than students who go to bed late.
2. Exercise also has a big effect on grades. Determine to get plenty of rigorous exercise.
3. For great advice on a diet that contributes to wellness and academic performance, peruse the videos on www.nutritionfacts.org, which detail the scientific literature on nutrition.
4. With the guidance of your doctor, consider shifting your diet away from meat, dairy, junk food, and highly processed foods.

Chapter Nine

Resources

1. Put together a package of programs, apps, and websites that will help you in college. Use the resources mentioned in this chapter and look around for others.
2. Explore the tutoring and counseling options that your school offers, and then make use of them. Also, get to know professors and top students. Most will be happy to help you with almost any problem.

3. Get your professors to love you by sitting at the front of the class, showing respect to the professor and your classmates, and practicing proper classroom etiquette. Show unreasonable enthusiasm for the subject by asking the professor questions after class and forwarding relevant articles.

Chapter Ten

Productivity

1. Each morning, write down everything you need to do that day. After comparing these tasks with your academic and personal goals, create a priority list, starting with the most important task. By following this list, you will always get the most important stuff done.
2. Limit your time with passive entertainment—such as video games and movies—that aren't helping you achieve your goals.

Chapter Eleven

How to Enjoy College

1. Keep an open mind about what school to go to. Don't fall into the false choice of "it's the Ivy League or the college down the street." Take the time to find a school that perfectly fits who you are and who you want to be.
2. To get the most out of college and life, focus on beneficial activities. Enjoy decadent activities sparingly. Determine which enjoyable activities are most fulfilling to you by asking yourself which ones add to the world, improve the lives of others, and have the potential to bring you financial freedom.

3. You are a composite of the people you spend time with. Choose what kind of life you want to have by hanging out with people who already live that life.
4. Travel. There's a whole world of adventure out there. A great way to experience the world is to study abroad. Check with your school. If it doesn't have a study-abroad program, find a program that you can join.
5. Take a weekly Sabbath—a day in which you avoid all homework, work, and anything that commonly takes up your time. Go into nature; spend time with people you normally don't get to see. Do volunteer work. Go to church. Spend time with God. Then return to regular life rested and refreshed.

Chapter Twelve

Finding Work

1. Actions speak louder than words. Spend your college years accomplishing things so you'll have a body of work to prove that you're a "highly motivated people person."
3. Prove your worth by going the extra mile to impress your potential employers. Shock them with your knowledge of the company and your determination to prove that you're the best person for the job.
4. Skills are ways in which you contribute to a company. Focus your electives on classes that teach you concrete skills. For example, learn Photoshop, conflict resolution, a second language, lab skills, and so on.
5. Read great resources on careers and job-hunting, such as *What Color Is Your Parachute?* by Richard N. Bolles and *Think and Grow Rich* by Napoleon Hill.

Bibliography

Introduction

1. Jobs, Steve. *One Last Thing*. PBS.org documentary, 56.24. November 2011. http://www.pbs.org/program/steve-jobs-one-last-thing/.

Chapter One

1. Dempster, F. N. "The spacing effect: A case study in the failure to apply the results of psychological research." *American Psychologist* 43 (1988): 627-634. doi:10.1037/0003066X.43.8.627.

Chapter Three

1. Ian M. Lyons, Sian L. Beilock. "When Math Hurts: Math Anxiety Predicts Pain Network Activation in Anticipation of Doing Math." *PLoS ONE* 7, no. 10 (2012). doi:10.1371/journal.pone.0048076).

Chapter Four

1. Wolf Shenk, Joshua. *Lincoln's Melancholy: How Depression Challenged a President and Fueled His Greatness.* New York: Mariner Books-Houghton Mifflin Harcourt, 2006. Kindle edition.

Chapter Eight

1. Eliasson A.H., C.J. Lettieri, A.H. Eliasson. "Early to Bed, Early to Rise! Sleep Habits and Academic Performance in College Students." *Sleep and Breathing* 14, no. 1 (2010): 71-5. doi:10.1007/s11325-009-0282-2.

2. Amika Singh, Léonie Uijtdewilligen, Jos W. R. Twisk, Willem van Mechelen, Mai J. M. Chinapaw. *Archives of Pediatrics and Adolescent Medicine* 166, no. 1 (2012): 49-55. doi:10.1001/archpediatrics.2011.716.

3. Kuo P., A.F. Whereat, O. Horwitz. "The effect of lipemia upon coronary and peripheral arterial circulation in patients with essential hyperlipemia." *The American Journal of Medicine* 26, no. 1 (1959): 68-75. doi:http://dx.doi.org/10.1016/0002-9343(59)90328-6.

Made in the USA
Lexington, KY
30 June 2019